BETTER BUSINESS BUREAU®

Insider's Guide to Success

Starting an eBay Business

The Better Business Bureau

with Alice LaPlante

the**Planning**shop

Palo Alto, California

Better Business Bureau Starting an eBay Business: Insider's Guide to Success
©2007 by Rhonda Abrams. Published by The Planning Shop™

ISBN 10: 1-933895-02-0
ISBN 13: 978-1-933895-02-04
PCN: 2006935589

Managing Editor: Maggie Canon
Project Editor: Mireille Majoor
Cover and interior design: Diana Van Winkle

Bulk Discounts and Special Sales
Better Business Bureaus, corporate purchasing, colleges, consultants:
The Planning Shop offers special volume discounts as well as supplemental materials for BBBs, universities, business schools, and corporate training. Contact:
> info@PlanningShop.com
> or call 650-289-9120

The Planning Shop™ is a division of Rhonda, Inc., a California corporation.

Cover photos © iStockphoto.com/Edyta Pawowska, Oleksandr Staroseltsev, Sarah Reilly, Wilson Valentin, Andrea Gingerich

"This publication is designed to provide accurate and authoritative information in regard to the subject matter covered. It is sold with the understanding that the publisher and author are not engaged in rendering legal, accounting, or other professional services. If legal advice or other expert assistance is required, seek the services of a competent professional."
— from a Declaration of Principles, jointly adopted by a committee of the American Bar Association and a committee of publishers

Distributed by National Book Network

Printed in Canada

10 9 8 7 6 5 4 3 2 1

A Message from BBB President Steven Cole

Starting an eBay business is one of the most exciting entrepreneurial ventures you can embark on. Having a trusted source to guide you through the process means you'll run a business that fits both your lifestyle and your financial goals. That source is the Better Business Bureau.

The *Better Business Bureau Starting an eBay Business: Insider's Guide to Success* walks you through every step of beginning your own online enterprise—from understanding the real costs of an e-business to setting up compelling auctions to selecting pricing strategies to dealing with customers. Knowing what to expect, what to ask, and what to look for will increase your chances of running a profitable, hassle-free eBay business.

When you start an eBay business, you'll come into contact with many different kinds of businesses—suppliers, delivery services, technical support companies, and others. The BBB fosters trustworthy relationships between businesses and consumers, which means that during any step of this process you can check up on the companies and services you're doing business with. And the BBB provides extensive services for consumers, including free Reliability Reports, arbitration services, and best-practices standards, to name just a few. For more information, see pages v-vii or check our website at *www.bbb.org*.

This book will help you navigate the often confusing waters of starting an eBay business. We interviewed experts from nearly 400,000 BBB members to find out what you need to know, which pitfalls to avoid, and the best resources to use when starting your business. The expertise and experience of BBB members provide insights you won't find in any other book.

Steven J. Cole
President and CEO
Council of Better Business Bureaus

According to a recent Gallup poll, 85 percent of Americans prefer to do business with a BBB member. In this book, you'll get the same reliability, dependability, and impartiality that consumers have come to expect from the BBB.

What Is the Better Business Bureau?

Whether you're checking out a supplier's reputation, need help resolving a dispute with a local business, or want to find out more about a charity you're investigating, the Better Business Bureau (BBB) supplies both consumers and businesses with the information they need.

With more than 150 independent local bureaus across the United States and Canada, BBBs contribute in a wide variety of ways to their communities. Local bureaus compile Reliability Reports, track and respond to complaints about businesses, arbitrate disputes, maintain websites where consumers can research companies and learn about local issues and scams, and work to encourage businesses to commit to delivering goods and services with integrity.

With consumers' help, the BBB is usually the first national group to learn of problems in specific industries. The BBB was on the front lines of the automobile "lemon law" debate in the 1980s. Individual states got on board, and with the BBB's assistance, enacted "lemon laws" to protect consumers who purchase defective motor vehicles.

Through the BBB's national website (*www.bbb.org*) and local bureaus, the BBB helps consumers determine whether companies and services are reputable. The BBB does this in many ways:

1) Consumer Complaints (see page x for how to file a complaint)

2) Reliability Reports (see page viii for how to access these reports)

3) Dispute Resolution

4) Code and Performance Standards

5) Online Certification Programs

6) Articles and Videos

Dispute Resolution

The BBB offers a binding arbitration program to people and/or businesses in need of resolving a marketplace dispute. The BBB provides a professionally trained arbitrator who listens to both sides, weighs the evidence, and makes a decision about the dispute. (While most bureaus provide this as a complimentary service, some charge non-member companies.)

Code of Advertising

Protecting consumers from deceptive and unfair advertising is at the heart of the BBB's mission. The BBB publishes a Code of Advertising that all members must adopt. The directives contain very specific rules, including when it is and is not appropriate to use terms such as "free," "factory direct," and "list price."

What the BBB Isn't

1. The BBB does not protect its own. The organization produces reports on, and conducts investigations into, both member and non-member companies.

2. The BBB is not a government agency. It is a private, non-profit organization funded by membership dues and other support.

Online Business Reliability Certifications

For companies selling products and services online, the BBB provides an online certification program. The **Online Reliability Seal** means that a company is a BBB member, has met the BBB's Code of Advertising, has been in business for at least one year, and is committed to dispute resolution to address customer complaints.

Articles and Videos

The BBB website (*www.bbb.org*) contains more than 800 free articles on topics ranging from "Work at Home Schemes" to "Choosing an Assisted Living Facility." For a complete list of articles, go to *www.bbb.org/alerts/tips.asp*.

The BBB also produces educational videos on various businesses, services, and products. The content is developed through extensive research, interviews with industry leaders, and reviews of consumer complaints. For a complete list of videos, go to *www.bbbvideo.com*. The videos are available for purchase but can also be found at most libraries.

The BBB is supported by more than 400,000 local business members nationwide. It is dedicated to fostering fair and honest relationships between businesses and consumers, instilling consumer confidence, and contributing to an ethical business environment.

BBB Membership Requirements

To be a member of the Better Business Bureau, a company must:

1. Be in business at least six months

2. Pay annual dues, determined by the size of the company

3. Meet all relevant licensing and bonding requirements

4. Promptly respond to all customer complaints and make a good faith effort to resolve all complaints

5. Cooperate with the BBB to eliminate any underlying causes of customer complaints

6. Comply with decisions rendered through the BBB's arbitration programs

7. Adhere to BBB standards in its advertising and selling practices

8. Agree to use the BBB name and/or logo only in the manners specifically authorized by the BBB

9. Support the principles and purposes of the BBB and not engage in any activities that reflect adversely on the Bureau

10. Supply appropriate background information to the BBB

11. Have no unsatisfactory reports in its Bureau's service area

12. Cooperate with the BBB's efforts to promote voluntary self-regulation within the company's industry

13. Be free from any government action that demonstrates a failure of the company to support the principles and purposes of the BBB

How to Check on a Company

When you are determining which companies to work with when starting your eBay business, the BBB can help you investigate a company's past performance to find out whether any complaints have been lodged against it. This process is called a Reliability Report (*www.bbb.org/reports.asp*), and in 2006, the system offered Reports on nearly 3 million U.S. and Canadian companies.

Reliability Reports list each company's name, address, phone number, fax, and contact person's name and email address. They also show if, and how, the company has resolved past disputes and if any actions have been taken against the company and/or its principals by government agencies. The BBB posts three years' worth of complaints for each company.

Complaints cover advertising issues, contract disputes, billing/collection issues, operational practices, product problems, and a category labeled "undefined issues." For example, one company's Reliability Report contained the following information: "This company has an unsatisfactory record due to its failure to respond to one or more complaints from consumers. The Bureau processed a total of 415 complaints about this company in the last three years; 191 in the past year."

You may search for information on a company that isn't yet in the BBB database. The Bureau generally waits until it receives three inquiries before starting a file on a particular company.

If you don't have access to a computer, you can receive a hard copy of a company's Reliability Report by calling your local BBB.

Information, Please

The BBB received nearly 102 million requests for assistance and 49.1 million requests for Reliability Reports in 2006, a 19 percent increase over 2005. The largest number of requests concerned:

1. Mortgage brokers: 1,357,199

2. Roofing contractors: 1,339,490

3. General contractors: 1,150,769

4. Movers: 1,109,342

5. New car dealers: 897, 929

6. Work-at-home companies: 753,306

7. Home builders: 721,458

8. Construction & remodeling services: 702,473

9. Auto repair & service shops: 691,793

10. Plumbing contractors: 602,741

How to File a Complaint

W hen a company says something in its ads that isn't true or sells you a product that doesn't work and refuses to fix the problem even after you've complained, what can you do? Some of us would stew about it, maybe tell a few friends, and refuse to ever do business with that company again. But you *can* take action (and help other consumers) by filing a formal complaint at *http://complaint.bbb.org.*

The BBB launches investigations, sometimes in conjunction with law enforcement agencies, whenever:

1. There is a pattern of inquiries or complaints about one particular company, and especially when there is a large number of inquiries or complaints

2. A company's offer is unusual or suspicious, is large in dollar value, or affects a vulnerable group (senior citizens, for example)

3. A company's principals will not cooperate with or provide the BBB with requested information

Because of this complaint system, the BBB is often the first organization to know about potential scams and troubling trends in particular industries. When a scam develops in one part of the country, the news travels quickly between BBB offices in the U.S., Canada, and Puerto Rico, and these offices, in turn, alert the media and the public. The BBB handled more than 1.2 million consumer complaints in 2006 and conducted nearly 11,000 investigations.

Once you've filed a complaint, the BBB will send a letter to the offending company to confirm that you truly are/were a customer and to get their side of the story. If you want additional information or need assistance with a complaint, please contact your local BBB, visit the BBB website (*www.bbb.org*), or call (703) 276-0100.

The Top Recipients of Consumer Complaints in 2006*:

1. Cellular phone services & supplies: 29,237

2. New car dealers: 23,380

3. Internet shopping services: 18,054

4. Furniture stores: 16,461

5. Banks: 15,250

6. Collection agencies: 14,463

7. Internet service providers: 14,353

8. Cable TV, CATV, & satellite: 13,394

9. Telephone companies: 12,371

10. Used car dealers: 11,225

*The BBB AUTO LINE program is counted separately. It handled 37, 434 complaints involving automobile warranty claims in 2006.

Note also that these figures represent actual complaints, not the larger number of requests for assistance and requests for Reliability Reports received in 2006.

About The Planning Shop

The Planning Shop, a nationally recognized publisher of quality books for entrepreneurs, is proud to publish the Better Business Bureau Insider's Guides to Success. The first three titles in the series are: *Buying a Home*, *Starting an eBay Business*, and *Buying a Franchise*.

The Planning Shop, located in Palo Alto, California, specializes in creating business resources for entrepreneurs. The Planning Shop's books and other products are based on years of real-world experience, and they share secrets and strategies from CEOs, investors, lenders, and seasoned business experts.

The Planning Shop's books have been adopted at more than five hundred business schools, colleges, and universities. Hundreds of thousands of entrepreneurs and students have used The Planning Shop's books to launch businesses and create business plans in every industry.

CEO Rhonda Abrams founded The Planning Shop in 1999. An experienced entrepreneur, Rhonda has started three successful companies. Her background gives her a real-life understanding of the challenges facing people who set up and run their own businesses. Rhonda is the author of numerous books on entrepreneurship, and her first, *The Successful Business Plan: Secrets & Strategies,* has sold more than 600,000 copies and was acclaimed by *Forbes* and *Inc.* magazines as one of the top ten business books for entrepreneurs. Rhonda also writes the nation's most widely circulated column on entrepreneurship and small business.

Successful Business Strategies appears on USAToday.com and Inc.com and in more than one hundred newspapers each week. Rhonda is also the small business columnist for Yahoo Finance.

The Planning Shop's other lines of books include:

The **Successful Business series**, assisting entrepreneurs and business students in planning and growing businesses:

- *The Successful Business Plan: Secrets & Strategies*

- *Six-Week Start-Up*

- *What Business Should I Start?*

- *The Owner's Manual for Small Business*

The **In A Day series**, enabling entrepreneurs to tackle a critical business task and *Get it done right, get it done fast*™

- *Business Plan In A Day*

- *Winning Presentation In A Day*

- *Trade Show In A Day*

- *Finding an Angel Investor In A Day*

Books published by The Planning Shop are available in bookstores across the country and online at *www.PlanningShop.com*.

Table of Contents

SECTION 1: PLAN YOUR EBAY BUSINESS

SECTION 2: GETTING STARTED

SECTION 3: CREATE COMPELLING LISTINGS

A Constantly Changing Landscape

" *If you see an opportunity to sell something and make it more affordable than people can get through other channels, then you have a potential eBay business. As for us, we sell anything we can purchase in large lots—from computers to clothing to tools, whatever. And although we've made some expensive mistakes along the way, we've managed to establish ourselves in the eBay community and have a strong customer base now. But we continue to learn, and our business model evolves every three months or so.* "

Robert Britton, BBB member,
eBay PowerSeller, and owner of Sterling Trading,
Whitmore Lake, Michigan

Plan *Your* eBay Business

Internet-Based Auctions

Y ou've heard about eBay—who hasn't? And you're understandably intrigued. So many people seem to be developing thriving businesses there. And whether you want to get rid of unwanted objects from your attic or garage, market one-of-a-kind items to savvy collectors, expand your existing retail storefront into an online operation, or purchase overstock from third-party manufacturers to resell at a discount, you believe there are tremendous opportunities to make money in the largest online marketplace on the planet.

And you'd be right. Today, eBay is a $42 billion company with $6 billion in annual revenues (in the 2006 fiscal year). In 2006, more than $52 billion changed hands within its virtual doors. The company's revenues are growing at a rate of 30 percent annually, and by the end of 2006 more than 82 million active users had bid, bought, or sold something

QUICK TIP

Buy Low, Sell ... as High as You Can

Because prices on eBay are extremely competitive—items typically sell for 30 to 50 percent of retail—you must be able to offer unique products or sell at very low cost. Otherwise, you'll never make a profit!

on eBay within the past 12 months. On an average day, more than 100 million items are up for auction. It's not surprising that you want to be a part of all this!

This book will walk you through the things you need to do to begin selling on eBay. Whatever your dream—to earn extra money to supplement your current income, or find a new career to support you and your family—you'll find the information and tools to get started.

A truly global marketplace

An auction is a specific way of selling. Rather than establishing a set price for an item, you offer it to whomever might be interested. Would-be buyers let you know how much they are willing to pay. The person who offers the most walks away with the item. It's as simple as that. But given that all this has been going on for thousands of years, why all the fuss about eBay?

One reason: scale. The Internet has created a global marketplace for the buying and selling of goods and services. Anyone with a computer and an Internet connection has the potential to join in.

Previously, your pool of buyers was much more limited. Let's say you had an idea for a business selling reconditioned laptops. Once upon a time, your options were to put ads in your local paper or advertise in the Yellow Pages. The number of people who would even know that your bargain computers were available would be extremely small.

But use eBay to try and sell those laptops, and you could get dozens—or hundreds—of buyers vying for your goods. And what a marketplace you've tapped into! Because the audience for your eBay auctions is the entire Internet-enabled world, the pool of potential buyers is limited only by the logistics (and costs) of delivering the goods.

The Most Efficient Marketplace

Theoretically, at least, an auction is the best way to determine the real value of a product. After all, when you set a firm price on something, you often don't know whether you've done a good job. You have clues, of course: if no one steps up to purchase your top-of-the-line Italian bicycles, you can assume the prices are too high. If throngs of people eagerly line up to buy them, you've probably offered them too cheaply. Only by asking multiple people what they'd personally be willing to pay—and letting them haggle amongst themselves in an auction—do you have a true measure of what the items are worth under existing market conditions.

The Rise of eBay

Originally called AuctionWeb, eBay was founded in 1995 by a computer programmer in the Silicon Valley who fervently believed in the commercial possibilities of a virtual auction block.

Today's eBay "community" of buyers and sellers is a fast-growing and loyal one. They are famously enthusiastic about the brand: more than 10,000 users show up every year for the firm's annual convention, called eBay Live. Since the majority of them are individuals paying travel and lodging expenses out of their own pockets, this devotion to what is, after all, a commercial entity, is indeed a phenomenon.

Entrepreneurs in record numbers are setting up shop on eBay, according to a survey conducted for eBay by ACNielsen International Research, a leading research firm. More than 724,000 Americans report that eBay is their primary or secondary source of income. In addition to these professional eBay sellers, another 1.5 million individuals say they supplement their income by selling on eBay.

The many faces of eBay

Who exactly buys and sells on eBay? The community is as diverse as the global population itself.

In the early days of eBay, the community consisted mostly of people who felt safe online, who were technically savvy enough to manipulate the tools provided, and who were mainly looking for computers, computer components, or other mechanical parts. There was also a very small, but active, group of collectible dealers who seized on the site early on as a way to reach their highly focused audiences.

That has all changed. The eBay site has become considerably easier to use and navigate, and even technical newbies feel comfortable there. The range of goods offered for sale is so varied that it cannot be adequately described here.

Although in the early days the eBay community was largely white, male, and American, this is rapidly changing. Currently, the community consists of people from all over the world, of all ages, interests, backgrounds, creeds, and nationalities. Today, eBay gets 50 percent of its revenues from outside North America. Whereas the number of U.S.–based listings increased nearly 20 percent in the second quarter of 2006, the compound annual growth rate of international sales was more than a whopping 120 percent.

On the buyer side, there are five main types of eBay users:

- Collectors looking for rare goods

- Consumers looking to purchase items that are difficult to find in their geographic area

- Consumers or businesses searching for products or parts that have been discontinued by the manufacturer

- Consumers who enjoy the eBay experience and like the convenience of shopping online

- Bargain hunters looking for deals on products that can easily be found in local brick-and-mortar stores but which are deemed too expensive to be acquired through those channels

As for sellers, the range of participants is vast. You'll find people selling items they found in their garages, people actively looking to acquire goods that they can then resell on eBay, people who have built entire eBay businesses on professionally sourcing items in bulk, people who create products that can't be found elsewhere, and people offering collectibles or other one-of-a-kind pieces.

It is getting harder and harder to generalize about the type of buyers and sellers frequenting eBay's electronic corridors. Pretty much anything goes—and everything does. Whatever you want to do, or whatever you want to sell, will almost certainly fit in.

From Ostrich Feathers to Power Boats: Today's eBay

Although the first items found on eBay were primarily electronics products and rare collectibles, the breadth of goods sold today will literally take your breath away—and fire your imagination about what's possible. Whether you have expertise in farm equipment and want to sell used John Deere tractors, know of a supply of 40-foot storage containers that can be mounted on railroad cars, or routinely acquire movie star memorabilia from Los Angeles estate sales, chances are excellent you will find a ready market on eBay.

How eBay makes its money

It's important to understand that eBay, like any traditional auction house, only *facilitates* the buying and selling of goods. It doesn't buy or sell anything itself. Instead, it makes its money by charging sellers fees for various aspects of the transaction and by offering so-called "value added" services, such as specialized graphics that make an auction listing look better or tools that allow you to research what similar items sold for over the past six months.

For example, you pay fees to list a product for auction and fees when the product sells, plus numerous optional fees based on factors such as how elaborate your listing is—whether it features boldface or colored type, for instance—and whether it includes photos. As of 2006, U.S.–based eBay transactions cost between 20 cents and $80 per listing, plus between 2 and 8 percent of the final price for an item. Additionally, there are a host of other eBay services, including research services and online store hosting services, which you may subscribe to and which could add even more to the total.

Of course, eBay is not the only online auction site. uBid, Webidz, Auctionfire, Onlineauction, Overstock.com, and Bid-alot offer alternatives, as do new heavyweight contenders Yahoo and Amazon—and many of these services offer free listings to sellers, choosing to make their money off a percentage of the sales price alone. To date, however, none of them has come close to rivaling the reach of eBay.

One of the reasons for this is the self-perpetuating nature of markets. In most cases, the bigger the market, the more opportunities exist for both buyers and sellers. Sellers want to seek out the greatest possible number of potential buyers; buyers want the greatest selection of goods. The more people participate in an auction marketplace, the more others want to join in. And as of today, the place to be is eBay.

The Dark Side of the Force

Despite all the advantages of online auctions, it's still buyer—and seller—beware. According to Harris Interactive, 35 million Americans participate in online auctions. However, a sobering 52 percent of sellers reported problems such as late payments, bad checks, stolen credit cards, and, especially, buyers who changed their minds after winning an auction.

According to the Internet Fraud Center, a nonprofit watchdog group, online auctions accounted for the most complaints about fraud—44 percent—with an average loss of $999 per transaction. Additionally, the Internet Crime Complaint Center at the FBI logged more complaints in 2006 about auction fraud than about any other type. A full 45 percent of the 200,000 complaints registered by the center involved auctions. And these complaints could come from either buyers or sellers. Buyers complain when they don't receive goods after they've paid for them, or because those goods were not what was represented. Sellers can be defrauded by buyers who attempt to pay for goods using stolen credit cards or overdrawn checking accounts, or who don't pay at all. So although the potential for profit is large, so is the potential for loss.

There are a number of reasons why this is the case. For starters, there are fewer safeguards on the Web for both buyers and sellers. Neither can see the other's face, so traditional methods of evaluating credibility and honesty are difficult to use. Sellers can go through all the bother—and expense—of an auction, only to have the buyer back out afterward. Not to mention that buyers don't see and touch the actual product, so they can be unsure about what exactly they are getting, and, rightly or wrongly, complain once the item shows up at their doorstep.

And none of this comes without a price. Most auction sites charge fees, sometimes hefty ones, to list an item. There are additional fees leveled once an item has sold. There are also shipping costs. And, of course, there all the usual expenses of being in business: the cost of the goods sold, your overhead, and your time.

Whether you can make eBay auctions pay off for you depends on a number of things: the market value of the goods you have to sell, your ability to effectively market those goods—and your own credibility—to the online community, and your ability to do all this efficiently and cost-effectively.

Your Business and Financial Goals

W hy have you decided to explore the possibility of starting an eBay business?

Service Matters

eBay customers have high expectations, and we need to be able to keep up with them. Inventory must always be available and ready to ship out, and you must represent everything as is. Because reputation is everything. We need to blow away our customers with great service.

Craig Smith, BBB member, eBay PowerSeller, and president and owner of AutoAccessory4u.com, Corona, California

Perhaps you've bought or sold things on eBay before, and you've seen that the eBay marketplace presents many opportunities for aspiring entrepreneurs. Perhaps you have a brick-and-mortar store, or you're a real-world manufacturer, and you recognize that eBay could be a vital additional sales channel for your goods. Perhaps you're an outstanding buyer of goods—whether cars, collectibles, or computers—and you want to find out if you can make a living buying and selling such goods on eBay, which offers you millions of potential customers in one place. Perhaps you want a flexible business—one that you can run on a part-time basis, from your home or while you travel—and you see that eBay is an outstanding platform for such an activity.

Whatever your motivation, your financial resources, or your time commitment, once you decide to run a business on eBay (not just clean out your garage or get rid of excess inventory), it's time to approach your eBay enterprise as a business. That means setting goals, establishing your business values, developing a business plan, and dealing with the day-to-day operations of running a business.

Business goals

What's motivating you to start an eBay business? Before you plan your business, it's helpful to articulate your motivations and goals.

Some of the many reasons to start an eBay business:

- **You have a low-cost source for a product.** You have access to an inexpensive supply of something that is continually in demand—perhaps you work with a supplier of lighting fixtures from Asia—and believe you can merchandise it well on eBay and sell it for more than it costs to acquire.

- **You're a creator of art, collectibles, or other unique items.** You want to find a larger market for the beautiful hand-crafted coffee tables you make than you can reach by advertising locally.

- **You're a manufacturer.** You make goods and want to find a new channel for selling your products in addition to your existing sales channels, if any.

- **You're a collector of rare items.** For example, you might have been collecting old coins since you were a child and now hope to cash in on some of your treasures.

- **You have a hobby that you want to turn into a business.** You may restore old clocks in your spare time. You realize that this hobby, if marketed correctly, could actually bring in an income.

- **You recognize an opportunity based on your day job.** You may have a day job in a particular industry and recognize a lucrative opportunity. For example, you could be a clerk in a fabric store and realize that there's money in selling remnants online.

- **You want to expand your brick-and-mortar storefront online.** You may already have a brick-and-mortar storefront and hope to build a business that goes beyond your local market to one that is national, or even international, in scope.

Hire Professionals

Every business benefits by having access to the services of an accountant or bookkeeper, especially in the early stages. Among their many valuable services, they'll:

- Set up your books

- Help you to understand financial terms and legal requirements

- Provide valuable advice on billing, payment, and payroll procedures

- Advise you about tax-saving strategies

- Assist with the financial components of your business plan

Business Goals

Use the worksheet below to help you clarify your motivation for starting an eBay business. Put a checkmark next to each of the goals you hope your eBay business will succeed in achieving for you.

GOAL	
Find a new outlet for items I am able to source inexpensively	☐
Find a larger market for my hand-crafted goods	☐
Have an additional channel for products I currently manufacture	☐
Find a way to make money from my collection of rare items	☐
Sell services I supply to the eBay marketplace	☐
Sell things I purchase from activities I enjoy, such as attending flea markets or shopping at garage sales	☐
Turn a hobby into a business by selling items associated with that hobby	☐
Take advantage of an opportunity based on my day job	
Add an online component to my existing brick-and-mortar business and reach the eBay marketplace	☐
Transform a brick-and-mortar establishment into an Internet-only business	☐
Use eBay as a marketing tool to reach a huge global market	☐
Other:	☐

Financial goals

Some new eBay entrepreneurs have ambitious goals. They hope to build their eBay presences into major businesses. They envision their companies clobbering the competition, defining new product categories, perhaps growing to a huge net worth. Or they have an existing business and they see eBay as an opportunity for major expansion, perhaps one day replacing their brick-and-mortar enterprise.

Others have more modest goals. They may just want to supplement their existing income from a traditional full-time job. Or, perhaps, they hope to eventually live on their eBay income, but recognize this will take some time.

By articulating your financial objectives, you can begin to come up with the basics for your business plan and a viable strategy for achieving your goals.

Financial Goals

Complete this worksheet, indicating your financial aspirations for your eBay business. If you plan on adding an eBay component to your existing business, indicate these numbers for the eBay portion of your business. Of course, at this point, these numbers reflect your hopes, rather than being based on solid research or planning. But clarifying them helps you to bring your goals into focus as you develop a business plan.

GOAL	ONE YEAR	THREE YEARS	FIVE YEARS
Annual eBay gross sales			
Annual eBay profits			
Annual take-home salary/draw from eBay activities			
Non-eBay business income (from business activities other than eBay transactions)			
Non-eBay employment income (from salaries or other employment)			
Other financial benefits from eBay activities (such as offsetting hobby-related expenditures)			
Other financial considerations			

Research, Research, Research

The single most important thing you can do before you start selling on eBay is to browse the listings, especially those in your particular market category. Interested in selling vintage dolls? Hang out in the Dolls & Bears category. Note each new listing as it is posted. Pay attention to the titles, subtitles, and descriptions of the listings. Pay special attention to the starting prices of auctions and how the bidding is proceeding. And once the auctions end, refer to one of the most valuable free tools that eBay provides: the Completed Listings search option.

Under the Completed Listings feature, you can see what a particular item—or class of items—has sold for in auctions that have ended in the last 15 days. This is priceless information. Not only does it tell you the ultimate price that bidders were willing to pay for certain items, but it gives you insight into the psychology of buyers in your particular category. Perhaps buyers of a certain kind of collectible wait until the last minute to place their bids—called sniping—which means that bidding stays at a remarkably low level until the last five minutes of the auction. Or perhaps buyers of certain kinds of consumer electronics are more likely to use the Buy It Now feature than bidders on other kinds of auctions.

In addition to the Completed Listings feature, which is free, you can subscribe to eBay Marketplace Research, which provides a great deal more information, plus tools that you can use to analyze auction results and buying patterns even more carefully. You can access up to 90 days' worth of historical data on completed auctions, as well as viewing charts that show average bids per auction, number of completed auctions, and more. You can also view top searches within each category to see what buyers are searching for within your particular market.

Develop impeccable business values

One of the main things you will discover as you begin selling through eBay is the importance of trust between buyers and sellers. It is vital for you to have the highest business ethics—and to be vigilant about maintaining them.

Building and retaining your business reputation is one of the most critical things you will do in any business. But eBay has built in a mechanism to measure this reputation—the feedback system—so the trust you build, along with your business values and ethics, are even more important in this environment.

Studies have shown that having even a small handful of positive responses from people who have been happy doing business with you via eBay can make a significant difference in how many people bid on your auctions and how much they bid. Indeed, a study performed at Stanford University in early 2006 showed that one extra bidder results in an 11.4 percent increase in revenues from a given auction. Proving to even one additional person that you are a reputable seller with whom it is safe to do business can make a huge difference to your cash flow. So:

■ **Always tell the truth.** On eBay, trust is everything. Because your buyers never see your face and never set eyes on the actual goods, they may be understandably leery about sending you their money. This is where the eBay community comes in—together, the 76 million active members keep an eye out for sellers who misrepresent their wares, fail to deliver the goods, or attempt outright fraud. Engage in questionable business practices, and your rating will plummet—and you will have trouble selling *anything* in the future.

■ **Say what you mean and mean what you say.** Be absolutely clear about what you are offering and the terms and conditions you will accept. Avoid any ambiguities at all costs—disappointed buyers will let the community know how they feel. Even if you inadvertently mislead a buyer through poorly written text or omissions, you'll pay the price.

- **Follow through on commitments.** On eBay, it is not enough to just have good intentions. If you say that you will ship the product in two to three business days, make sure you do it. All other assurances to the buyer must also be fulfilled precisely. Your rating depends on how well you live up to the commitments you make to sellers, not just the quality and price of the products you sell.

- **Be courteous and prompt in all communications.** One of the best things you can do to establish trust is to respond immediately to any inquiries, questions, or after-the-sale issues that come up. Your emails should be professional—with proper punctuation, correct spelling, and no slang or questionable language.

- **Make it right.** If buyers have even the smallest quibble with you, do everything in your power to keep them happy. No matter if the misunderstanding or problem originated on their end, "The customer is always right" should be your mantra.

QUICK TIP

Your Technology Requirements

Every eBay business is a technology-based business. So, having the appropriate technology is essential to your success. Some of the basic categories of technology you will need:

- Computer
- Virus protection
- Internet service provider
- Office software, including word processing
- Accounting/bookkeeping/tax software
- Digital camera
- Telephone/cell phone
- PDA—Personal Digital Assistant or mobile pocket Internet device (optional)

Collecting Sales Tax

Many people wrongly believe that Internet sales—including sales made on eBay—are not subject to sales tax. That is not true. Here's what you need to remember: most *products* sold to *end users* in the *same U.S. state* as the seller are subject to *sales tax*, whether they are sold in a store, online, or from a catalog.

States call sales taxes by various names: sales tax, franchise tax, transaction privilege tax, use tax, and more. Sales tax rates and rules vary from state to state, county to county, city to city.

■ **Products:** Sales tax is levied on the sale of most *products*—every state has its own exemptions, which often include food, prescription drugs, animal feed, and sometimes clothing. A few states also tax some *services.*

■ **End Users:** Tax is collected when a sale is made to the *end user*. Products sold for resale (to other stores, for instance) or to be used as raw material for the manufacture or creation of other products to be sold to end users are generally not taxable.

■ **Same state:** The U.S. Supreme Court has twice ruled that states cannot require businesses to collect sales tax unless the business has a *physical presence* in the same state as the buyer. But *physical presence* is broadly defined. If you have ANY location, facility, employee, call center, address, or even one independent sales person in a state, you have to collect taxes in that state. So, if you are running your eBay business from your home in Virginia, but storing and shipping that inventory from a warehouse in Maryland, then you must collect sales tax on sales to customers from both Virginia and Maryland.

Typically, collecting sales tax is the responsibility of the seller. On each taxable transaction, you calculate the applicable sales tax, collect it from the buyer, keep tax records, file a tax return, and pay the taxes to your state. You'll pay monthly, quarterly, or annually, depending on your level of sales. You generally need to get a license from the state to begin to collect sales tax.

For an excellent resource on state tax rates and rules, check The Sales Tax Clearinghouse (*www. thestc.com*). You'll find the latest information covering online sales tax policy, a link to your state's taxing authority, subscription services to make calculating sales tax easier if you are doing many online transactions, and, of particular help, a Lookup Rates link to help you find the sales tax—state, county, or local—for any address in the U.S. Be *certain* to ask your accountant for help with sales tax issues.

The Home-Based eBay Business

T he vast majority of the sellers on eBay work out of their homes. Even after they experience a great deal of financial success, many eBay sellers prefer to work at home because they need to be there (they may have young children or be the primary caregivers for elderly relatives), because they don't want the expense of maintaining a separate store or office, or simply because they prefer to work from their homes.

But running an eBay business from your home—like running *any* business from your home—takes thought and careful consideration. Most eBay businesses involve *products*, which means you'll have to have the space to store, ship, and receive inventory. Moreover, you are almost certainly going to be doing business with a large number of people you've never met—and will never meet—so you may be concerned about the safety and security of sharing your home information with strangers. It takes thought and planning to successfully run an eBay operation from your home.

Types of home-based eBay businesses

There's a wide range of options for the *types* of eBay businesses that are best suited to being operated out of a home. These can range from inventory-based businesses, such as purchasing goods for resale, to creative businesses, such as making fashion items or crafts, to repair or restoration businesses, such as restoring old watches. It may also be possible to run home-based eBay businesses in which you do not take any possession of goods; perhaps you will be able to sell services rather than goods or, if you are fortunate, perhaps you will be able to locate goods from other parties that you can sell but are not required to take possession of—for instance, sourcing batteries from a manufacturer who ships directly to the purchaser.

Successful home-based eBay businesses share many of these characteristics:

- **Little or no foot traffic.** There are usually strict zoning laws about businesses run out of the home. In most cities, an area zoned as residential has to follow some very specific rules about what is and isn't permitted on the premises. One of the most common provisions of local zoning laws is a limit on traffic in and out of the home.

- **Light or moderate deliveries**. As with foot traffic, vehicle traffic should not be too intrusive in a residential neighborhood. Daily deliveries from commercial shipping services (such as UPS or FedEx) may be acceptable, but deliveries involving very large trucks or industrial vehicles may not be permissible on your street and may be against zoning laws.

- **Inventory is easily stored, managed, and shipped.** If you are selling large quantities of goods, you must have adequate storage space to accommodate your inventory. Your merchandise should also be relatively easy to organize, access, and ship. If your business requires storing large quantities of oversized or bulky items—like pool tables or widescreen TVs—you should consider a solution other than a home-based business.

- **Inventory is not exceptionally valuable.** Security is always an issue when you deal with very expensive items. You probably won't want the risks of stockpiling pricey items in your home, as that may make your premises more vulnerable. So if you deal with valuable items—such as jewelry with precious gems, high-end collectibles, or antiques—you'll need to do business, or at least manage storage and shipping, from a location more secure than your home.

■ **Few employees are required.** Unless you have a very large house with dedicated office space, it is difficult to run a home-based business with more than two or perhaps three employees. Not to mention that it might be against local zoning laws.

■ **Adequate technological infrastructure is available.** Although more and more people have access to broadband for quick Internet access, as well as electronic voicemail and other more sophisticated communications technology offered by telecommunications companies, some regions are still dependent on dial-up Internet connections or telephone service that doesn't offer value-added features like voicemail, call waiting, or conference calling. Make sure these kinds of services are available before starting your eBay business from your home.

Income Tax

Any money you receive as a result of selling something must be accounted for as income according to state and federal tax laws. However, you can deduct as expenses anything related to running your eBay business. If you need to travel—whether across town, across the country, or even overseas—for your business, all the costs you incur will be considered expenses and reduce your income taxes accordingly.

The best way to find out about how taxes will affect your business is to talk to an accountant. You can also go to the IRS website (*www.irs.gov*). Here you can download forms and learn about taxpayer identification numbers, payroll taxes, and everything else related to running a business. And once you reach a certain size, you'll probably need an accountant to help you keep track of everything—especially if you hire employees.

Depending on your income, the types of products you sell, and other issues concerning the way you run your business, you'll be able to deduct some of your business expenses. Some of these may include:

■ Equipment

■ Office supplies and services

■ Car

■ Travel

■ Entertainment

Life/work balance

One of the biggest misconceptions that many people have about eBay is that the auctions and sales will take care of themselves. The truth is that setting up and running successful eBay sales can eat up significant chunks of time. For starters, you have to acquire the items to sell. Although at first you may only list stock you already have on hand, eventually you will run out of inventory and you will need to replenish your supply.

Even if you currently enjoy spending time finding products (say, going to flea markets to acquire collectibles), when you must continually do this for your business, you may find it becomes more of a burden than a diversion.

Also, you will need to pay attention to how you create your listings. Rather than just throwing together a title and a brief description, you must take care to come up with text that accurately describes what you are selling, making it sound enticing without misrepresenting it. You'll need to devote time to taking excellent photographs of your wares—or pay someone else to do it. These little things matter a lot when people are deciding whether or not to bid on your items. And they all take time.

You will also get inquiries and questions from prospective buyers, and it's important to answer these in a timely manner. Not only do you need to get back to the interested person before your auction ends, but often if you don't answer them within an hour or two they will have moved on—and you will have lost their business. Most new sellers are surprised by how much time it takes to interact with potential buyers.

Once a sale is made, you have to communicate with the winning bidder, process payment, and package the product for shipment. All of this takes time, as well. And if you have not arranged for pickup, you'll have to take the shipment to the post office or shipper's office.

And your work isn't done yet. You'll still have to deal with any follow-up from the sale, including questions from the buyer, or—in the unlikely event that something goes wrong—any complaints or problems that arise. On top of that, you'll have to take care of the purely administrative aspects of your business—bookkeeping and bill paying, paying taxes, maintaining records, and the like.

If that sounds like a lot, you're right. Which is why many people who start off with the vision of making a lot of money working just a few hours a week quickly find the demands on their time actually encroach significantly on their personal lives once they start making regular sales. Inevitably, one question you will have to answer is: How much of my time am I willing to devote to this business?

How Much Time Will eBay Take?

Use this worksheet to estimate how much time you are willing to spend each week on your eBay business. Once you get your business started, track how much time you are actually spending and see how the two compare.

ACTIVITY	TIME SPENT PER WEEK (ESTIMATED)	TIME SPENT PER WEEK (ACTUAL)
Researching eBay		
Acquiring or creating products		
Creating listings		
Taking photos of products		
Uploading information to website		
Answering emails from customers		
Finding and purchasing packaging materials		
Packaging goods		
Trips to and from the post office, FedEx, UPS		
Processing payments from customers		
Bookkeeping and accounting		
Other		
TOTAL		

Turning a hobby into a business

There's nothing more attractive than the thought of taking an activity you love—photography, or cooking, or collecting Asian antiquities—and turning it into one that can earn you extra money or even support you entirely. But despite all the get-rich-quick and work-at-home advertisements you see, it's no easier to do this on eBay than to open a traditional store in your own town center. The same business precepts apply. If you are thinking about turning your hobby into an eBay business, be sure to:

■ **Do your research.** As with any other business, you're going to have competition. Look at what is already available and at the prices that competitors are able to command for their products. Chances are good that there are dozens of people already living your dream. There might be room for you in that market—or there might not be. Use eBay's Completed Listings search feature (see page 14) to determine whether the market will bear your particular brand—or price point—of wares.

■ **Evaluate your work ethic.** There's a big difference between doing what you love in conjunction with your normal work and personal activities, and devoting a lot more—or all—of your time to it. Some people find that their hobby is actually a lot less enjoyable when they have to practice it all day, every day. Think carefully about what you are willing to do to make your hobby-turned-business venture a success.

■ **Estimate your true costs.** You may knit the most exquisite scarves in the world, but if the wool alone costs you $100, and you also need to factor in the value of your labor, you may end up selling at a loss in the competitive eBay space. Make a thorough analysis of *all* the expenses you accrue—*including* the cost of your time—to make sure that eBay will actually be a profitable venture for you.

■ **Determine your suitability to make sales.** It's a fact: some people just don't like selling. They find it distasteful to have to praise their own products or services or promote themselves in any way. Perhaps the largest part of being successful on eBay is enjoying "the game." It can be very exciting for the right personalities—but very uncomfortable for others. You need to decide which camp you belong in.

Getting the Right Insurance

Once you have substantial inventory or other property, you should consider getting proper insurance to protect your goods. If you are working from your home, you might, wrongfully, assume your home insurance covers all losses. There are often limits on how much you could recoup if you were robbed or some other disaster befell your home. Your insurance company could also cancel your policy if it discovers that you are using your home for business and you try to file a claim related to that business. Home-based businesses require special insurance.

Some of the basic types of insurance coverage you should consider:

■ **Contents insurance.** How much would it cost you to replace your computer? Your fabric cutter? The materials in your darkroom? Also, if you have business equipment you routinely use, such as a laptop computer, cell phone, or PDA, you may need to get a special rider to cover these items.

■ **Business interruption insurance.** Say your premises catch on fire, are flooded, or are damaged by an earthquake. Business interruption insurance will protect you from losing money when you cannot conduct business as usual.

■ **General liability insurance.** Although homeowners' policies will cover anything related to your personal life, they won't protect you if an employee or business visitor (say a delivery driver) gets injured on your premises. If you routinely have people come to your house for business purposes, you should consider purchasing this kind of policy.

■ **Additional car (or truck) insurance.** If, as is likely, you use your car for business purposes (even if you're just going back and forth to the post office) and want to deduct your mileage on your income tax return, get your car insured for business use.

■ **Product liability insurance.** If you sell a product on eBay, you might want to purchase product liability insurance. This protects you if a buyer sues you because your product harmed them in some way or didn't perform up to your claims.

Bricks and Clicks: Expanding a Business onto eBay

W hen most people first think of eBay, they envision sellers cleaning out their garages to make more room or selling their old electronics for a few extra bucks. In reality, eBay is a thriving marketplace for those who also do business in the non-virtual world—through brick-and-mortar stores or traditional distribution methods.

eBay presents two main advantages to those who are considering adding an online component to their existing businesses: it is relatively easy to get a business up and running and eBay already has a huge market of potential customers who participate in the eBay experience.

eBay can be a great tool for expanding an existing business, but if that is your goal, you need to understand: 1) what you have to offer eBay, and 2) what eBay has to offer you.

What can you offer eBay?

The most successful eBay bricks-and-clicks businesses are those that offer either specialized products or services or those that offer a distinct price advantage. Probably the best strategy is to distinguish yourself by offering something that is very difficult to get elsewhere. Say you design and sell socks of every imaginable color, in all sorts of materials and designs. You already have a successful storefront. You also sell through department stores and other retail outlets. And you want to expand to eBay. You actually have a good shot at it, because of your uniqueness. Buyers will find few other merchants offering exactly what you've got for sale.

Or perhaps you sell a product that is quite commoditized, like used printers. There are many eBay businesses that sell refurbished used printers at attractive prices. So how do you move from your quite profitable brick-and-mortar storefront and distinguish yourself sufficiently on eBay to make money? You do it by specializing in a particular manufacturer and emphasizing your expertise in your item descriptions. You also provide extraordinary after-sales warranty and support.

Competitive pricing is another way to distinguish yourself from other sellers. This strategy works best when you have access to an extremely low-priced source of inventory that is not readily available to competitors. Otherwise, a low-price position strategy is a difficult one to maintain in the world of eBay. eBay is a notoriously price-competitive marketplace—and others generally have access to the same

Quick Tip

Bricks and Clicks

A company that does business both online and in the traditional, non-virtual, brick-and-mortar world is sometimes referred to as a "bricks-and-clicks" business.

sources of inventory as you. Even if you find a source of inventory at an extraordinarily low cost, chances are good that competitors will eventually catch up with you. You cannot count on running a long-term business based on one or two sources of low-cost inventory.

Having an existing brick-and-mortar storefront presents a couple of disadvantages in comparison to starting an eBay store from scratch. First, you're likely to have more fixed overhead expenses than someone who runs a completely virtual business. That might make it difficult for you to compete on price alone. Also, you'll need to keep an eye on whether you are creating conflict with your other sales channels if you are seen to be selling the same products at a lower price online.

What can eBay offer you?

The fact that eBay has already attracted so many previously existing businesses indicates that, for many, there are clearly advantages to selling in the eBay environment. Some entrepreneurs, however, think of eBay or other online auction sites as an afterthought—a place to turn to when times are slow or to get rid of excess inventory.

But simply putting items on eBay is not a plan for success. Rather, it's best to think of eBay as another *channel* through which you can distribute your goods or services. Managing any sales channel takes time, effort, financial commitment, and planning. The same is true of eBay.

Developing an eBay component to your business offers clear advantages. You can:

■ **Expand your market by opening up this new channel.** This is the No. 1 reason for expanding your business to eBay. You might feel constrained by the limits of your local market. The demand for handmade dolls could be limited in Lincoln, Nebraska. Listing your products or services on eBay gives you access to national or even international markets.

■ **Get rid of overstock.** You could, of course, have a fire sale at your retail store. But you may be able to get better prices for last year's fashion items or excess inventory of Christmas goods by offering them on eBay.

■ **Test out new product ideas.** One of the best things about eBay is that the community will let you know instantly if there is a demand for what you have to sell by voting with their dollars. At relatively low risk—by purchasing just a few items from your wholesale source— you can test the waters to see whether there's a market for a new product or service that you can then sell in your brick-and-mortar storefront if there's sufficient demand.

■ **Leverage existing infrastructure.** You already have the inventory, the computer systems, the telecommu- nications services, and the business cards/stationery to support your existing brick-and-mortar business. Going online means you don't need to invest significantly in additional infrastructure to expand your market reach. If you're successful, of course, your costs will increase. But already having everything in place to do business means you can start out slowly with virtually no risk at all.

Of course, taking on the added responsibilities of doing business on eBay brings additional challenges, as well. You might:

■ **Lose focus.** If you're running a business now, chances are you're already working overtime to meet the current demands of your operations. Adding an online channel might distract you from your core money-making activities, not to mention increase your stress levels exponentially.

■ **Increase costs without increasing revenues.** Although you might have infrastructure in place to run your business, there are inevitably additional costs to expansion. You might have to hire additional employees to manage your eBay listings, for example. Or pay for additional computer equipment or upgrade your telecommunications infrastructure. And you might do all of this without reaping the revenues you'd hoped for.

- **More competition.** Sure, you have access to a dramatically bigger marketplace. But you also have more competition. *Lots* more competition. Although you might have been able to charge a premium for your product or service in your local market due to scarce supply, that's unlikely to happen on eBay unless your product or service is unique indeed. Before you expand your business online, make sure that your business model supports potentially rock-bottom sale prices.

Brick-and-mortar to bricks-and-clicks

If you have an existing business in the "non-virtual" world (sometimes called *terrestrial* or *real* world), how do you know when it's a good time to start doing business on eBay?

Existing businesses have a number of advantages over other novice eBay sellers when launching on eBay, including:

- You are already buying inventory and have some inventory to begin with immediately.

- You have established sources of supply; you know which suppliers have unique merchandise or particularly good prices, and perhaps you are already going on buying trips or attending trade shows.

- You know the current wholesale prices and typical profit margins and mark-ups on goods in your industry.

- You already have the business infrastructure in place—bookkeeping, computers, administrative help, warehousing, and perhaps even technical assistance.

- You know and understand the market and what customers want.

- You approach your business as a *business*. Many eBay sellers do not understand the commitment it takes to make a profit over time.

Your business is likely to be a particularly good match for eBay when:

■ Your customers upgrade their products regularly, you offer a buy-back program for their used merchandise (as with autos, technology products, and sports equipment), and you have more used products than you can easily sell or you don't want those used products in your store.

■ Your customers lease products from you and you need an outlet for their used merchandise (as with technology products, industrial equipment, and office furniture).

■ You have seasonal merchandise you must clear out regularly and want to reach a wider market than you could with only in-store sales (for instance, fashion, beach/pool supplies, snow blowers, sports equipment).

■ You are located in a very small or limited market area, or your market is shrinking, and you do not have enough customers where you are, even though there is strong nationwide demand for your products.

■ You want to sell products that are different from or unrelated to what you're currently selling, without confusing your current customer base or opening another physical store.

■ You can add eBay activities without adding staff. This is particularly true if you have technically adept employees who have extra time that could be used to build and maintain your eBay presence.

■ You have technically adept family members (daughters, sons, nephews, nieces) who will build and maintain your eBay presence in return for merchandise, low pay, or their allowance. (Many eBay sellers use family members to help them.)

■ You have a lot of excess merchandise you have been paying to keep warehoused.

Online Staffing

No business expansion comes without costs. In the case of expanding to eBay, you will almost certainly have to put in more hours than when you were running your traditional business only. Although some business activities won't change—you will still be sourcing and managing inventory, for example—you'll also have to write the listing descriptions, take photos, upload the listings to eBay, and administer the auctions with as much care as if they were your sole business.

This may require you to put in extra time yourself. But as every businessperson knows, time is already a precious commodity and can be difficult to find. Your employees are also, more than likely, stretched to the max. You may have to hire additional personnel to manage the eBay part of your business. Although this will likely involve only part-time help at first, if your eBay transactions take off, you could find yourself needing to ramp up even further.

An entire industry has sprung up to provide services for eBay merchants. Rather than hiring extra employees, you may possibly be able to get some of the help through outsourcing some tasks. Check the Solutions Directory on the eBay home page to see the range of services available to assist you.

Business Basics

No matter what type of eBay business you're thinking of starting—full or part time, home-based or
based in an office or warehouse, as an adjunct to an existing
business or as a brand-new endeavor—you're well advised
to spend a bit of time putting together a business plan.
Business plans are critical for any business, but for eBay
businesses they are particularly helpful. Many of your eBay
competitors probably started without much planning, so
having a thoughtful plan for your business can give you a real
edge. Make sure your eBay business plan builds in flexibility,
because on eBay, markets change quickly.

A business plan is a road map that will help to guide you as
you start and grow your business. The critically important
part of a business plan is not the document itself, but the
planning *process*. Developing a business plan gives you the
opportunity to think through the key issues that will contribute to your long-term success and to consider the challenges you're likely to face.

QUICK TIP

A Great Plan—Quick!

If you do not have a business plan yet, it's time to develop one. *Business Plan In A Day*,
from The Planning Shop, provides you with a step-by-step, easy-to-use guide to crafting a
thoughtful business plan quickly. It includes a sample business plan to help walk you through
the process. *Business Plan In A Day* is available in bookstores throughout the United States
and Canada, as well as from The Planning Shop at *www.PlanningShop.com*.

As you develop your business plan, you'll be examining the following questions:

- Does my basic concept make sense?

- Is there a clear-cut market need for my product/service?

- What advantages do I have over my competition?

- Are my financial projections realistic?

- Is this business likely to succeed? Why?

Understanding your target market

A critical part of your plan is clearly identifying and defining the characteristics of your potential customers. Your success rides on your ability to meet the needs and desires of the *types* of customers you expect to serve. They are your target market. Your goal is to ensure that:

- These customers do exist on eBay.

- You know exactly who they are and what they want.

- There are enough of them to support your business.

- They're ready for what you have to offer and will actually bid for it when you list it in an auction.

Even if you already have an existing business and feel you have a good grasp of the characteristics and needs of your customers in your business, you may have a somewhat different customer base in the online world.

Understanding the competition

No matter what type of business you own or are planning to start, other companies want your customers. The fact that competition exists means you have tapped into a viable market with customers who want to buy the goods or services you have to sell. That's why other businesses, like yours, want to profit from them. Understanding your competition proves you can:

- Distinguish your eBay business from others.

- Identify factors that will make customers choose to bid on your offerings over others.

- Respond to needs that aren't currently being addressed by competitors.

- Figure out what you're up against and be prepared to tackle competitive obstacles to your success.

Operations plan

How are you actually going to run your eBay business? The Operations section of your business plan briefly describes how you will execute the basic functions of your company: acquiring or creating your product or service, keeping on top of inventory, and delivering your product/service to your customer.

You should emphasize any operational features that give your company a competitive edge. If you've found a way to cut costs and increase profit margins by using less expensive suppliers, highlight those aspects in your business plan. Your goal in this section is to show:

- You've thought through what it takes to make your eBay business function easily.

- You are capable of managing those functions on a day-to-day basis.

- The reasons for any changes, and additional costs, in operations if you already own a brick-and-mortar store—and what those changes will do for your profit margins.

Your Business Structure

If you are not already in business—or if you are setting up your eBay operation as a separate entity from your existing company—you'll eventually need to decide on a corporate structure for legal and tax purposes. Be informed about your options—and be prepared to be flexible, as your needs will probably change as your business grows.

- **Sole Proprietorship.** Most people start their businesses in this corporate form. As the name implies, you are the sole owner of the business and take full responsibility for all its activities. It is the most basic structure, and the simplest to manage from a tax point of view. Because you own the business personally, all your income (and related expenses) are included on a separate schedule on your personal income tax return. But there is a major drawback to this business form: with a sole proprietorship you will be *personally* liable for any legal judgments against the business. For this reason, many sole proprietors who grow to a certain size transform themselves into corporations (see below).

- **Partnership.** Under this structure, two or more people share the responsibilities and ownership of the business. If you begin working with another, the law may impute a partnership whether or not you have drawn up a formal agreement. However, it is strongly advised that you have a written partnership agreement, overseen by attorneys, if you are going into any partnership.

- **Corporation.** The main advantage of the corporate form is that it gives a company's owners personal liability protection. In other words, the owners' personal assets cannot be seized due to a court ruling or business debt. However, corporations cost more to set up and maintain than a sole proprietorship or LLC.

- **Limited Liability Company (LLC).** An LLC provides one of the most important benefits of a corporation—protecting the owners from personal liability—without many of the legal complications of being a corporation.

Focus on the Basics

"*When you're starting out, you want to keep it simple. Keep your eye on the basics. Pick something to sell that you feel is unique, that a lot of other people don't offer. Anything that can differentiate you or your products is a plus.*"

Stella Kleiman, BBB member,
eBay PowerSeller, and owner of FoundValue,
San Francisco, California

SECTION

2

Getting
Started

eBay Basics

Though the range and scope of eBay keeps expanding, there are a few general types of businesses that thrive there:

- **Second-hand reseller.** You are the classic eBay seller: you have items that have been hanging around in your attic or garage, or you haunt other people's garage sales and purchase used goods from them at bargain prices. You then take these items and offer them up for auction.

- **Bulk reseller.** This is another common type of eBay seller. You buy goods in bulk for cheap, then put them on eBay hoping to make a profit. Items that fall into this category include overstocks from clothing or linen manufacturers, discontinued items, or large lots of hardware goods such as nails, nuts, or bolts. Usually the profit on these individual items is small—sometimes very small indeed—but over time the money adds up.

- **Collector/Trader.** The name of this category speaks for itself. You have a passion for something and either collect it yourself—which is how the majority of these kinds of sellers start out—or routinely purchase items because their rarity makes them a good investment.

QUICK TIP

Finding Your Niche

Deciding which category your goods belong in can make the difference between briskly ringing up sales and waiting for bids that never come. You'll want to list your items where those who are searching for them can find them, but it won't always be obvious where your items belong. Many buyers search by product category—or even subcategory—so carefully peruse the other items that appear in a particular location before listing your product there.

Coins, stamps, pottery, and watches fall into this category, as do any number of other niche items.

- **Standard retailer.** If you're this kind of seller, you're just like the shopkeeper in a traditional brick-and-mortar business. In fact, you very likely have your own retail storefront. You buy from wholesalers and resell to the public, hoping for a healthy margin on what you sell. eBay is another sales channel for you.

- **Arts and crafts maker.** A growing number of sellers create their own goods—ranging from furniture, dolls, and original photographs to jewelry, perfumes, soaps, and even paintings—and auction them off to the highest bidder.

- **Consignment reseller.** These are becoming more common and involve a seller who takes on responsibility for selling other people's goods online in exchange for a commission or other kind of fee. Over the past few years, a number of "drop-off" eBay consignment businesses have opened up around the country. People who don't have the technical skills or inclination to sell on eBay themselves designate others to do the work for them.

eBay PowerSellers

PowerSellers are those eBay sellers who have been active members for more than 90 days, average at least $1,000/month in sales for three consecutive months, and have a feedback rating of 98 percent or higher on at least 100 total feedback submissions. Membership is free. You cannot apply for it—eBay invites qualified members to join via email.

There are several advantages to being a PowerSeller:

- **Better customer service from eBay.** Your emails or phone calls are given priority by eBay customer service representatives over those from non-PowerSellers.

- **Access to the PowerSeller-only discussion board.** This is a valuable source of information on marketing, sales, and fulfillment activities from your fellow PowerSellers as well as eBay representatives.

- **Special offers.** Vendors regularly offer, exclusively to PowerSellers, special promotions of products and services designed specifically to help eBay sellers.

Pros and Cons of eBay Businesses

TYPE OF SELLER	PROS	CONS
Second-hand reseller	Selling extra things from your house reduces clutter and makes you money.	Unpredictable supply. What happens when you've sold everything in your house?
Bulk reseller	You can buy low and sell high!	High upfront costs of buying in bulk.
Collector/Trader	Limited number of collector's items means a smaller supply and less competition, which could allow for premium pricing.	Difficulty in acquiring collectibles or rare items at a low cost.
Standard retailer	All the pros of being in a traditional retail storefront: you're your own boss; you can potentially make a lot of money; you set your own hours and decide exactly what you will sell.	All the risks of being in business for yourself: products might not sell or might not sell at a profit; overhead may be too high; the amount of time it takes to run the Internet store can exact a toll on your professional life and be very stressful.
Arts and crafts maker	Make money selling your personal creative output. Lead the artist's life.	Large amounts of time often needed to create the products. Frequently, the prices at which you can sell your goods are not high enough to justify the huge investment in hours. Also, it may be hard to create sufficient volume to make a business worthwhile.
Consignment reseller	Unlimited source of supply.	Difficulty in marketing yourself to people with things to sell in order to ensure a steady stream of products. Challenge of being able to charge a high enough fee to make the sales worth your while.

Ways to sell

No matter what type of business you are in, what items you sell, or where you get them, you have a variety of options for selling on eBay. You can settle on one particular sales strategy or try a combination of several—whatever works for you.

- **Standard auction.** The basic, most common way to sell an item on eBay. This format lets you list an item for sale, collect bids for a fixed length of time, and sell the item to the highest bidder.

- **Buy It Now.** You have the option to offer a Buy It Now price that allows a buyer to purchase an item immediately at a price you set. Sellers can offer the Buy It Now feature in *standard auction* and *store inventory* formats. If they attain a certain ranking score, they can also offer it in a fixed price format (see page 144).

- **Best Offer.** You can choose this option when offering Buy It Now listings so that buyers can suggest a price they are willing to pay for that item. This feature allows sellers to receive price-based offers from buyers which can be accepted at their discretion. Once a buyer makes a Best Offer, you can choose to do one of the following:

  - Accept the Best Offer and close the listing.
  - Decline the Best Offer and tell the buyer why the offer was rejected.
  - Allow the offer to expire on its own in 48 hours (the offer will also expire when the listing ends).
  - Respond with a counteroffer.

- **eBay Stores.** Beginning in 2002, eBay began offering technical infrastructure (including hosting fees, shopping carts, and other features), as well as other services, so that sellers could easily set up their own online stores. This allows you to consolidate all your auctions in one place and get to know your buyers much more intimately. You'll find, for example, that as you gain a reputation for selling quality goods and delivering superlative customer service, you'll get repeat customers and your auctions will generate more money. Monthly subscription fees for setting up an eBay store range from $15.95 per month for the most basic store that does little more than list your items and link to the actual auctions, to $499.95 per month for the most sophisticated storefronts, which include customized checkout procedures, tools to send out email newsletters to favorite customers, and the capability of listing hundreds of items. Stores can be easily customized to have the look and feel you desire, and once you set one up, you can feature items you are offering in eBay standard auctions as well as ones you are selling at fixed Buy It Now prices.

- **eBay Express.** In mid-2006, eBay opened its eBay Express site, which operates like a standard online store to sellers with U.S. addresses. These are not auction sites, but Buy It Now-only deals, where the seller has set a firm price that buyers can take or leave. One advantage to sellers is that buyers can purchase items from multiple eBay Express sellers without having to go through a checkout procedure and approve payment for each one separately. In effect, as a seller, you offer your buyers the convenience of shopping in an online "mall" with thousands of other vendors. However, there are strict requirements that must be met before a buyer can open an eBay Express store: for starters, you must have a feedback score of 98 percent or higher based on at least 100 buyers' input. You must also be a U.S.–registered seller, and the items you are selling must be located in the United States. All listings must include photos and specify shipping costs upfront.

- **Want It Now.** If buyers are having trouble finding you, or if you want to get ideas for what you can sell on eBay, you might want to investigate the Want It Now option. This is where buyers tell sellers exactly what they are looking for. You can then contact the buyers posting the notices and directly offer your wares for sale.

Ways to Sell on eBay

TYPE	KEY FEATURES
Standard Auction	■ Buyers bid on items
	■ Bids are collected for a fixed time
	■ Can have "reserve" or minimum price
Buy It Now	■ Buyers can purchase items immediately for a set price
	■ Auction can occur simultaneously
Best Offer	■ Buyers can offer a price
	■ Purchase is immediate
eBay Stores	■ Gives you more buyer recognition
	■ Consolidates your auctions
	■ Gives you more buying tools
eBay Express	■ For experienced sellers
	■ Gives you a "storefront" for Buy It Now items
	■ Easier checkout for buyers
Want It Now	■ Lets you find buyers who are looking for exactly what you've got

Market categories

eBay is organized according to market category. Choosing an appropriate category is very important to your selling success. That's because when buyers log onto eBay, the first thing they see is the blank Search box where they can describe precisely what they are seeking to buy. Right next to it is a place where they can specify the category. This means that instead of searching the entire, very large site for, say, Vera Wang wedding dresses, they can tell the system to search only in the Clothing, Shoes & Accessories category. This results in a much faster search and makes sure that superfluous items don't pop up on the Search Results page.

Spend time familiarizing yourself with the eBay categories. Look at listings of products in categories related to those you might want to sell. This will not only help you find the best category—or categories—for your listings, but will give you a sense of the marketplace, what sells, and what type of competition you have.

Like any marketplace, eBay has its own methods of organization, and you need to understand them. Do vintage dresses sell in Clothing, Shoes & Accessories or Collectibles? Does Tickle Me Elmo sell in Toys, or Dolls & Bears?

You have 34 market categories to choose from:

- **Antiques.** One of the most popular eBay auction categories, you can list anything from musical instruments, to carpets, ethnographic items, and, of course, furniture.

- **Art.** Here you can sell everything from traditional oil and watercolor paintings to prints, sculptures, drawings, mixed media, and photography.

- **Baby.** Everything related to babies: cribs, strollers, car seats, clothes, diapers, formula, and just about anything else you can think of.

- **Books.** eBay Books & Magazines has books of all types and genres, both used and new, fiction, nonfiction, textbooks, antiquarian books, children's books, and, of course, more magazines than you ever knew existed.

QUICK TIP

Get the Category Right

If you don't choose an appropriate category for your item, eBay will move your listing. So it's best to do the work yourself and pick the right category; otherwise, you might be assigned one that isn't the best for promoting your particular auction item.

How Bidding Works

eBay automates a great deal of the bidding process for buyers, making it easy for them to bid on and track auctions. This is good news for sellers, too: because it is so easy for buyers—not just to place the initial bid, but to stay on top of the auction so as to not get *out*bid—they are prone to bid more frequently, and higher.

There are just three steps to placing a bid:

1) From within the item listing, the buyer clicks the Place Bid button.

2) They enter the maximum amount they are willing to pay for that item (they can increase this later if the bidding exceeds that amount and they wish to continue participating in the auction).

3) Review the bid, and click the "Confirm Bid" button.

That's it! eBay will then bid on behalf of buyers, up to the maximum amount they specified. The bidding will increase *automatically* in increments based upon the last bid received for the item. For example, say a buyer is bidding on a vase where the current bid is $10, and they have specified a maximum bid of $25. If someone else submits a bid for $11, eBay will automatically submit a bid on the first bidder's behalf for $11.50. If another bidder tops that, then eBay will automatically bid 50 cents more on the first bidder's behalf, up to $25.

CURRENT PRICE	BID INCREMENT
$ 0.01 – $ 0.99	$ 0.05
$ 1.00 – $ 4.99	$ 0.25
$ 5.00 – $ 24.99	$ 0.50
$ 25.00 – $ 99.99	$ 1.00
$ 100.00 – $ 249.99	$ 2.50
$ 250.00 – $ 499.99	$ 5.00
$ 500.00 – $ 999.99	$ 10.00
$ 1,000.00 – $ 2,499.99	$ 25.00
$ 2,500.00 – $ 4,999.99	$ 50.00
$ 5,000.00 and up	$ 100.00

■ **Business & Industrial.** This is a heavy-duty category, where many of the items listed go for tens of thousands of dollars. The category includes business, agricultural, construction, and industrial equipment.

■ **Cameras & Photo.** This category is appropriate for anyone from the photography neophyte to the most experienced professional. You can sell digital cameras, 35-mm cameras, camcorders, memory cards, and accessories here.

■ **Cars, Boats, Vehicles & Parts.** Also called eBay Motors, this category includes everything from cars and trucks to RVs, Jet Skis, motorcycles, and boats.

- **Cell Phones & PDAs.** Here you can sell new or used devices and parts.

- **Clothing, Shoes & Accessories.** One of the most popular categories on eBay, Clothing, Shoes & Accessories features clothes and accessories for women, men, and children alike.

- **Coins & Paper Money.** Whether you cater to amateur or professional collectors, here's where you can ply your currency wares from around the world.

- **Collectibles.** This has been a big-selling category since eBay's earliest days. You can sell everything from Disneyana to comics, vintage clothes, books, and trading cards here.

- **Computers & Networking.** Found a source or steady supply of new or used laptops, desktops, or accessories? Here is where you go to auction them off.

- **Consumer Electronics.** A major category for sellers dealing in new and used iPods, TVs, home entertainment systems, and car stereos, among other consumer electronics.

- **Crafts.** Whether you sell supplies or finished craft products, this is where you would list your items.

- **Dolls & Bears.** A specific category broken out of the general Crafts category, this is for specialty sellers of dolls and bears—both new and used.

- **DVDs & Movies.** Used DVD and VHS titles move quickly on eBay. Whether you are trying to get rid of items from your personal library or you systematically buy up used titles from video stores that are reducing or eliminating inventory, this is the category to go to.

- **Entertainment Memorabilia.** Here you can list both popular and hard-to-find memorabilia from the entertainment industry, including autographs, and movie, television, and video game collectibles.

- **Gift Certificates.** If you are a reseller of coupons for anything from books to movies to garden supplies, this is the home for your listing.

- **Health & Beauty.** Believe it or not, eBay is the No. 1 site for purchasing health and beauty supplies. You can sell everything from cosmetics to makeup, perfume, skin care, and health products here.

- **Home & Garden.** Just what it sounds like. List furniture, appliances, and fixtures here.

- **Jewelry & Watches.** Not surprisingly, this is a particularly robust category, and you can list inexpensive as well as pricey jewelry and watches here. Vintage *and* new items sell briskly.

- **Music.** No matter what format your music items are in—cassette, LP, CD, MP3, or 45 or 78 rpm record—you can ply your wares here. Buyers are looking for everything from rock to classical, R&B, rap, jazz, and country music. Bootleg recordings are not permitted.

- **Musical Instruments.** This category features all types of musical instruments, for students, amateurs, and pros, along with audio equipment for concerts and other gigs.

- **Pottery & Glass.** Another subcategory of Collectibles that was broken out into its own area because of its popularity, this category is where you would list glass, pottery, porcelain, and other items, both new and vintage.

- **Real Estate.** This category reflects a new phenomenon: people buying homes, commercial buildings, and vacation timeshares over the Internet.

- **Specialty Services.** It's true that eBay isn't limited to product auctions. You can sell services ranging from advice and instruction to artistic talents to eBay support services to help others sell.

- **Sporting Goods.** A category that has been growing steadily in popularity in recent years, this is where you list everything from athletic clothing to equipment ranging from mountain bikes to fishing gear to golf clubs.

- **Sports Memorabilia, Cards & Fan Shop.** Another collectibles category that has burst forth on its own, eBay's Sports Memorabilia, Cards & Fan Shop is where you would list items such as autographed baseballs, trading cards, and sports souvenirs.

- **Stamps.** Whether you want to go into business selling stamps from the U.S. or around the world, this is a vibrant marketplace.

- **Tickets.** Whether you possess tickets to a sporting event, music concert, or cruise, you can sell them on eBay—however, there are some very strict guidelines around ticket sales online. (See page 49 for more.)

- **Toys & Hobbies.** If you have access to a supply of either new or vintage toys, this is the place to set up auctions to reach potential buyers.

- **Travel.** A relatively new eBay category, this is where you can sell (or resell) railroad tickets, car rentals, cruises, and vacation packages.

- **Video Games.** Because this category boasts such a huge selection, many gamers flock to eBay, making it an excellent place to list either new or used titles.

- **Everything Else.** This final, catch-all category includes everything that can't be squeezed into any of the other categories—everything from historical maps to metaphysical or religious products, gift baskets, wedding supplies, and even caskets.

Selling Tickets on eBay

eBay permits the resale of tickets to entertainment events—including sports, musical concerts, and theatrical productions—but only under some strict guidelines. After all, there are stringent laws regulating the sale (and resale) of tickets that vary from state to state.

There are several different eBay ticket-selling policies based on the type of tickets you are trying to auction off.

- **Primary ticket sale policy.** So-called "primary" ticket sales can be freely listed. A "primary sale" means that the ticket is being sold by the artist or organizer of the event in question.

- **Ticket package policy.** Ticket "packages" may be listed on eBay as long as they don't offer buyers the option of purchasing the tickets as stand-alone items. Instead, the tickets must be sold as part of a larger deal that can include such things as a backstage pass, participation in the event itself, or travel to and from the event.

- **Resell ticket policy.** Sellers listing event tickets for resale cannot accept any bids above the total face value of the amount printed on the ticket, except when specifically allowed in some states. The seller must end the auction when this price is met.

Violations of any of these policies can result in the cancellation of the listing, limits on account privileges, account suspension, or any combination of the above.

QUICK TIP

Listing in Two Categories

eBay allows you to list your item in two categories. Although it will cost more, doing this can pay off in spades by attracting more potential buyers to your auction. Sellers can list in any two categories across the site except adult items, real estate, capital equipment, and multiple-line (or Dutch) auctions.

What you can't sell

In its earliest days, eBay was essentially unregulated. But as eBay grew, it found it necessary to restrict or forbid auctions for various items. Some of the restrictions relate to eBay.com (the U.S. site), while other restrictions apply to specific international sites (for example, Nazi paraphernalia is forbidden in Israel and Germany). Regional laws and regulations may apply to either the seller or the buyer. Among the hundred or so banned or restricted categories are the following:

- Tobacco (tobacco-related collectibles are allowed)

- Alcohol (alcohol-related collectibles, including sealed containers, as well as wine sales by licensed sellers, are allowed)

- Drugs and drug paraphernalia

- Bootleg recordings

- Firearms and ammunition

- Used underwear and dirty used clothing

- Teachers' editions of textbooks, including home-school teachers' editions

- Human parts and remains

- Live animals

- Certain copyrighted works or trademarked items

- Lottery tickets, sweepstakes tickets, or any other gambling items

Take a Tour of eBay

T he moment you log onto eBay (*www.ebay.com*), you'll notice that everything is geared toward the *buyer*. This is as it should be. In fact, you should be happy about this. As a *seller* of goods, it's to your advantage that everyone who enters the virtual storefront in order to buy can quickly and easily find their way around. You'll notice that there are special promotions, featured products, and featured categories, all geared toward enticing buyers to purchase goods.

Although the home page is constantly changing, there are some basic features that always appear. The first one you will notice is that you are continually encouraged to "sign in." This means entering your user name and password and officially identifying yourself before the site will allow you to do anything other than simply browse listings or look up help items. As a seller, you will need to sign in before you list an item for sale or check on the status of an auction.

Of course, before you can sign in, you must establish an eBay account. If you haven't done so already, do so now. It's free, and you can accomplish it in less than a minute. Just click on the Sign In button that you'll find at the top of any eBay page, and follow the directions to establish your own account.

While the look of the eBay home page changes daily, the main features always remain the same.

Here's an overview of the main features you'll find on the eBay home page:

Main Menu Bar

At the very top of the page is the main menu bar. It offers five basic tabs: **Buy, Sell, My eBay, Community,** and **Help.**

- **Buy.** This takes buyers to a page listing all the resources for them. They'll be given a search field (see below) through which they can search for specific products by keywords, plus a prominent list of categories. They'll also be provided with links to a broad range of support reference materials that will help make their shopping experience with eBay safer and more productive.

- **Sell.** This is the primary "door" through which you will enter eBay as a seller. The first page that appears will invite you to describe the item you have to list; it also walks first-time sellers, step by step, through the selling process. As you become more proficient at selling, you will move quickly past this page to other, more sophisticated tools.

■ **My eBay.** Click on this link, and you'll be invited to sign in. Then, up will come a list of all your buying and selling activities. This is very convenient for keeping track of your listings and for monitoring which of your auctions have closed—and for how much.

■ **Community.** This is your portal to one of the most important aspects of belonging to eBay: the community. This is the universe of everyone who participates in the eBay marketplace—both buyers and sellers. In this completely open marketplace, your actions are transparent to everyone—and you will be given feedback on how well you have lived up to your commitments. Study after study has shown that the sellers with the highest satisfaction ratings not only sell more, but sell at higher prices than those who have not pleased their customers as well. Under the Community tab you'll also find discussion boards, where you can join in online chats on everything from participating in specific categories to learning how to best market yourself and your auctions to how to participate effectively in international auctions. (For more on the eBay Community, see pages 68-73.)

■ **Help.** eBay prides itself on its Help feature. It is concise, easy to understand, comprehensive, and covers just about everything you could want to know about buying or selling on eBay. You can search by keyword or you can browse Help topics alphabetically. The top questions people ask about eBay are also prominently listed so that new buyers or sellers can get up to speed quickly.

Search Field

Probably the most important aspect of eBay's home page is the Search field at the top of the page. This allows buyers to search for specific items by typing in words that describe what they are looking for. They can narrow down the search further by looking only in a particular category—for example, they can type in "inkjet cartridge," and then specify Computers & Networking to the right of that. This means that only those listings that have both the words *inkjet* and *cartridge* listed in their title or descriptive text *and* which are in that particular category will show up on the Search Results page. (This is why it is so important for you to describe your products clearly and use the keywords that buyers are looking for in your listings.)

Categories

Another key attribute on the home page is the Categories list on the left-hand side of the page. By clicking on one of these categories, buyers will be shown a list of subcategories; for example, after choosing Business & Industrial they will be able to select from subcategories that include Agricultural & Forestry, Construction, and Manufacturing & Metalworking. By clicking on any of these subcategories, buyers will be taken to an even more specific list of groups. Buyers can then narrow down their areas of interest quite specifically before browsing through particular auctions—which only underscores the importance of listing your goods in the correct category in order to attract the most, and most appropriate, buyers.

Specialty Sites

These links take you to the alternative sites within eBay that encompass traditional auctions, as well as:

- **eBay Express.** These operate like standard online stores. These are not auction sites, but Buy It Now-only deals where the seller has set a firm price that buyers can take or leave.

- **eBay Motors.** This specialty site focuses solely on automotive products: cars, trucks, RVs, motorcycles, boats, and all related parts. Otherwise, eBay Motors functions the same way as eBay—you photograph, describe, and post an item, choose an auction time period, determine whether you will conduct an auction and/or sell it through Buy It Now, and list it.

- **eBay Stores.** Special pages on eBay featuring all the items offered by an individual Store seller.

- **eBay Business.** A specialty site within eBay that provides tips, tools, deals, product discounts, and services you need to manage and grow your business when buying and selling on eBay.

- **Half.com.** Sell books, CDs, video games, and much more at set prices. Sellers are individuals and small businesses who sell directly to buyers.

- **Apartments on Rent.com.** One of the more recent additions to eBay is Rent.com, which allows people to view homes and apartments to rent.

- **StubHub.** StubHub brings together buyers and sellers of tickets for live entertainment events. The main difference between StubHub and a regular eBay auction of tickets is the cost: buyers and sellers each pay a significant percentage of the final negotiated price to StubHub for using the service. However, the breadth of choice available on StubHub as compared to regular eBay ticket auctions is such that many would-be ticket buyers go there to find tickets to the events they want to attend.

The Sell page

The most important link for sellers is at the very top of the page. It's the Sell link in the menu bar.

Click on the Sell link to go to the main Sell page.

By clicking on the Sell link, you'll get to the main Sell page, which has a number of important features. Most prominently, there's the blank space in which you are prompted to type in a description of what you have to sell (see page 57). By doing this, you will be guided to pick the right category for your item.

In addition, you'll see other features, such as a step-by-step walk-through of how to list an item for sale on eBay, a list of the top buyer searches, and a link that allows you to browse categories to see where items that are most like yours are being listed.

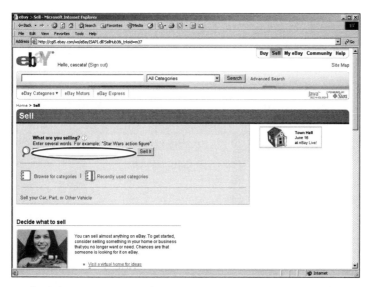

To find the right category for an item, type in a description of what you're offering on the main Sell page.

If you go online immediately, you'll notice that many of the features listed on this page require you to have a seller's ID and password before you can proceed. (Learn how to register and get these all-important credentials on page 64.)

Navigating by category

Buyers can navigate their way around eBay—and therefore find your auctions— in two ways. The first is to click on a category—and, usually, a subcategory—and browse through the listings that appear there.

There are both advantages and disadvantages to you (the seller) when a buyer proceeds in this way. On the plus side, those who search by category for something to buy are the equivalent of window shoppers in a brick-and-mortar store (or a garage sale or flea market booth). Sure, they aren't as completely focused as they would be when looking for a very particular item—whether it's a stainless steel frying pan, industrial sewing machine, or Malibu Barbie. But on the other hand, many thousands of dollars in sales are made every day through impulse buys, when shoppers didn't necessarily set out to purchase a specific product but ended up forking out money to acquire it anyway.

The disadvantage when buyers peruse your wares in this fashion is that the best potential customers—the people who really, *really* want that lava lamp—might be distracted by the huge number of listings in a category and have trouble finding your particular needle in this very large haystack.

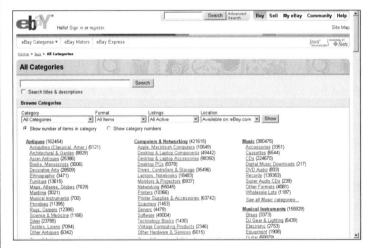

Shoppers who browse by category will have hundreds of headings to choose from.

Navigating by search

The other main way for buyers to find your listing is through a keyword search. This is just what it sounds like: They enter a description of what they are looking for in the blank field at the top of the home page. The more words they enter, the narrower their search will be. Thus, "Dell WiFi laptop" will get fewer, but more accurate, hits than "laptop"—which in turn would yield fewer hits than simply typing in "computer." (The fewer the hits, the better for you the seller, as buyers are homing in on your goods.)

Buyers can specify whether they wish to search throughout all of eBay or only in a specific category. Additionally, they can specify whether they want to search for the keywords in the item title alone, or in the title *and* listing description. Generally, they will get more hits if they search in both.

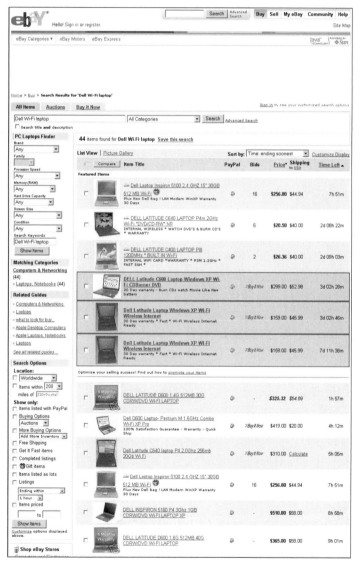

A keyword search will deliver a results page like this.

The auction screen

Once buyers locate an item they are interested in investigating further—either by clicking on a listing that has been displayed through navigating by category or by searching using keywords—the primary auction screen appears. This contains a wealth of important information provided by you, the seller.

An auction screen.

The buyer will see:

■ **Current bid.** This lists the current highest bid on the item.

■ **End time.** When you list an item for auction, you are asked to specify the date and time that the auction will close. After that point, no more bids will be accepted, and the highest bidder will be deemed the winner of the auction.

■ **Shipping costs.** The cost (usually charged to the buyer) of shipping the item.

- **Ships to.** Where you are willing to ship the item. Although some items can be shipped internationally, many are too large or bulky to travel economically beyond the borders of the United States and Canada.

- **Item location.** Where the item is physically located.

- **History.** Who within the eBay community has bid on this item, when, and for how much. You'll see their eBay User IDs, not their email addresses, which are kept private unless buyers decide to disclose them to you.

- **High bidder.** The user name of the eBay member who is currently the highest bidder.

- **Watch This Item.** Allows an interested buyer to stay on top of the bids for a particular item. Updates can be sent via email, text messaging, cell phone, or IM. Many people use this feature to track how fast the bids are piling up for an item they are interested in, with the intention of *eventually* bidding for it. When a buyer waits until the last possible moment to submit a bid, this is called *sniping* (see page 151).

- **Meet the seller.** Provides the buyer with critical information about you, including your name, feedback (expressed as a percentage of positive feedback received from people who have previously purchased items from you), and feedback comments. There's also a button to click that lets a potential buyer email you with any questions, and one they can use to view any other items you might have listed for sale on eBay.

QUICK TIP

eBay Prompts to Bidders

When a potential buyer places an item on their "watched" list or submits a bid, eBay sends out emails to remind them when the auction is drawing to an end or when they have been outbid. This is one way eBay helps sellers out by encouraging buyers to bid—or bid higher.

- **Listing and payment details.** Includes the starting time and date of the auction, the starting bid, the duration of the auction, and the preferred payment methods, whether PayPal (see page 66), personal check, money order, cashier's check, or any combination of the above.

- **Description.** This is the all-important text in which you describe, as precisely as you can, what your item is. You should be as exhaustive as possible, detailing the dimensions and important features such as color, condition, function, and maker. Use of photos—the more the better—is highly recommended.

In addition to all this, many sellers include a frequently asked questions (FAQs) section (see page 154) that discusses such things as warranties, refunds and returns policies, the standard processing time before an item is shipped, and other details that will help buyers decide whether or not they want to bid on the item.

QUICK TIP

Be Direct in Your Listing Title

Because some buyers will only search through listing *titles* when trying to locate an item, make sure that your title is very specific about what you are trying to sell. Don't try to be cute. Just tell the world simply and clearly what you have to sell. Thus, "Vintage 1950s metal lamp" is better than "Amazing lighting fixture bargain!" Use words that buyers would use to describe your item in your listing title.

The Importance of Feedback

Your feedback rating, expressed as both a number and a percentage, is visible at the top of the auction screen for every item you sell. Your feedback is made up of what buyers have said about you. You receive:

- +1 point every time one of your buyers says something positive about you.

- 0 points if you receive a neutral comment.

- –1 point for each negative comment.

In addition, the *number* of people who have left comments about you is listed.

For example, **Jonathan (340) 98.8% positive** means that 340 buyers have left feedback comments for Jonathan, and 98.8 percent of them were positive.

Having a good feedback score from a large number of buyers is the No. 1 thing you can do to boost your credibility as a seller. Not surprisingly, buyers tend to trust those sellers who have the longest track records (that is, who have sold the most items) and who have managed to satisfy the vast majority of their customers.

Getting to the point where you have a fair number of positive comments can take time for a new eBay seller. There are no tricks; you simply need to sell as many goods as possible and deliver superlative customer service. If a customer complains, make sure you resolve their problem immediately—or you'll almost inevitably get a negative comment. This can be deadly, especially when you are starting out (see page Chapter 29 for more on feedback).

Registration

The very first step in starting an eBay business is to become a registered seller. This is very easy. Indeed, eBay's most attractive attributes are the ease of use of its interface, the quality of its online help, and the expertise of support staff who are ready and waiting to answer any of your questions. But before you can begin to sell on eBay, you have to register for a seller's account.

Click on any of the functions on the sellers' main page (go to the main eBay page and click on the Seller link at the top of the page, or go directly to *http://cgi5.ebay.com/ws/ eBayISAPI.dll?SellHub3Visitor*) and a Register button will appear to prompt you that you need to become a member before proceeding further.

Once you find the Register button, click on it. You'll see a form that you need to fill out (see page 65). It's easy, and best of all, it's free. Being registered as an eBay seller gets you into important parts of the site that you'll need to become familiar with.

QUICK TIP

Register Immediately

Even if you don't plan to sell anything quite yet, register as a seller. You won't have access to key seller sections of the eBay site until you do. And it's best to start familiarizing yourself with what's available to help you sell your wares—whatever they might be—as soon as possible.

The form you'll fill out to register on eBay.

To register, you'll need to provide your name, address, phone number, and email address. Then you'll choose an eBay member name and a password.

The most difficult part of the process will be choosing an appropriate eBay member name. That's because, with so many millions of buyers and sellers, the most obvious names have already been taken! You may have to be creative to come up with a unique one that also reflects your business. If you're having trouble, eBay can suggest a member name for you. Just ask by clicking on the designated button.

Make PayPal Your Payment Pal

The best advice I can give you for protecting yourself against fraud is to use PayPal for online payments. It's now worldwide, and any good bidder will use it right away.

Jim Nieciecki, BBB member,
eBay PowerSeller,
and owner of Federation Toys,
Hoffman Estates, Illinois

QUICK TIP

Contacting Customer Support

If you have a question at any time that cannot be answered by the entries in the eBay help pages (*http://pages.ebay.com/help*), you have two ways to contact eBay. The first is by email: on every help page there is an Email Us icon as well as a Contact Us option. Both will allow you to submit your query to eBay customer service representatives. If you are anxious for a faster response, you can use the Live Chat feature, which will link you directly to a customer service representative in real time.

PayPal: Your Key to eBay Transactions

PayPal is an eBay subsidiary that offers a system that lets buyers make payments to you via the Internet. As an electronic alternative to traditional ways of paying, such as checks or money orders, a PayPal payment for your auction is guaranteed to be legitimate—and it's frequently preferred by buyers over credit cards because of the concerns many have about giving credit card information to strangers over the Internet.

When buyers register for a PayPal account, they provide a credit card and/or bank account number. When they wish to pay for an item, they log onto PayPal, provide their user name and password, and enter the email address of the seller. PayPal then charges their credit card or debits the funds from their bank account. In effect, PayPal acts as a secure clearinghouse for transactions. Rather than having to give their personal information out to multiple sellers, buyers provide it once to PayPal, which then processes the transactions and deposits the funds into the sellers' own PayPal accounts. Sellers then have the option of transferring the funds from their PayPal accounts to their own bank accounts or requesting a check from PayPal.

Registration for a PayPal account is easy for buyers: they simply provide their name, choose a user name and password, then type in their credit card number, expiration date, security code, and billing address—just as they would when purchasing anything online or over the telephone—*or* they provide a bank account number from which funds will be withdrawn when purchases are made. Upon doing this, the PayPal account is immediately viable.

If you want to sell on eBay, you need to apply for a Premier or Business account. Registration is just as straightforward as for buyers; the only difference is that you are required to enter a number for a bank account that is affiliated with the PayPal account.

- **Premier accounts** are for anyone who wants to accept payments for eBay transactions as well as purchasing items. Among other benefits, this account allows you to accept payments from unverified PayPal members via their credit cards; get instant access to any money in your PayPal account via bank transfer, ATM withdrawal, or check; and get seven-day-a-week customer support.

- **Business accounts** provide all the benefits of a Premier account as well as allowing you to do business under a company, rather than individual, name and accept payments from customers without PayPal accounts.

For buyers, PayPal offers 100 percent refunds against any unauthorized payments sent from buyers' accounts, as well as providing dispute resolution services, and a $2,000 Buyer Protection guarantee for many eBay purchases.

For sellers, a PayPal account provides the following benefits:

- **Protects against fraud.** PayPal has a staff of fraud experts who search continuously for suspicious activity on your account. If anything occurs that seems out of order, PayPal notifies you immediately.

- **Offers buyer complaint mediation.** PayPal has a mediation process that helps buyers and sellers resolve any disagreements about a transaction.

- **Prevents unwanted "chargebacks."** A chargeback occurs when a buyer asks a credit card company to reverse a transaction that has already cleared. The two most common reasons for chargebacks are a credit card being stolen and used fraudulently to make a purchase, and a buyer disputing the transaction because they are dissatisfied with it. Precisely because PayPal is so proactive about monitoring potentially fraudulent activity and offers a mediation structure, chargebacks are less common than when a seller accepts credit cards directly from purchasers.

PayPal is free for the buyer—there is no fee for sending a payment via PayPal. For sellers, the fee schedule is as follows:

ACTIVITY	PERSONAL PAYPAL ACCOUNT	PREMIER/BUSINESS PAYPAL ACCOUNT
Open an account	Free	Free
Send money	Free	Free
Receive PayPal payments funded by the buyer's credit card or debit card	4.9 percent, plus 30 cents (USD) — limit of five transactions per 12-month period)	1.9 percent to 2.9 percent + 30 cents (USD)
Multiple currency transactions	Exchange rate includes a 2.5 percent fee	Exchange rate includes a 2.5 percent fee

Getting Involved

Because eBay doesn't sell any products itself but makes its money from what you sell, it's in the company's best interest to help you succeed. Not only does this increase the pool of sellers in the marketplace; it in turn attracts more buyers and strengthens eBay with each new member who signs on.

To that end, there are a number of helpful resources in place, many of them free, to help teach you how to become a better—and more effective—seller. All these resources can be found at *http://hub.ebay.com/community*.

- **Workshops.** These are interactive online events led by eBay staff or expert eBay members. They are presented as text events—that is, you attend by reading what the moderators and other attendees are saying on your screen and participate by typing in questions or comments. You log on at a specified day and time and can either attend silently or participate actively. Should you miss the live version, past workshops are archived and can be accessed at any time. Past workshops include

QUICK TIP

Time: Your Most Important Investment

All sellers agree: the more involved they get in the eBay community—participating in the forums, attending the classes at eBay University, and going to the town meetings—the more quickly they get up to speed on how to make their eBay businesses successful.

"Use Research to Find the Best Time to List," "Put Last Year's Slam-Dunks to Work for You," and "Advanced Marketing Strategies."

- **Mentoring Groups.** This is an interactive program for new eBay members to help them learn how to sell. The people hosting the groups are volunteer members of the community who are donating their time and knowledge to help others. There are more than a dozen different mentoring groups for new sellers, depending on the exact subject you are interested in.

- **eBay University.** This is a collection of online training courses that you complete at your computer, on your own time and at your own pace, and are designed to help you sell more effectively. Courses range from Selling Basics—which explains how to open a Seller's account, do research, and create listings, and open and use a PayPal account—to more advanced courses on subjects including how to create compelling listings, how to use eBay tools, and how to open and market an eBay store

  In addition to the online courses, eBay offers on-site courses around the country led by live instructors trained by eBay. To find a course near you, go to the main eBay University page (*http://pages.ebay.com/university/index.html*), and under the "Find more classes in your neighborhood" link, type in your city and state—or, alternately, your zip code—and you'll get a listing of the classes in your area.

- **"eBay Radio with Griff" and "Ask Griff."** Jim Griffith, or "Griff," the dean of eBay University, has two online radio shows where you can learn more about eBay. Every Tuesday from 11 a.m. to 2 p.m. Pacific time is "eBay Radio with Griff"; on Sunday from 3 p.m. to 5 p.m. Pacific is the "Ask Griff" show, which invites buyers and sellers alike to call in and ask any questions they have about eBay.

Become a Mentor

Interested in becoming a Mentor? Eligibility to volunteer as a Mentor requires, among other things, 99 percent positive feedback and a total feedback score greater than 50. You'll first need to join the eBay Volunteer Program.

■ **Community Answer Center.** You can get help from other eBay members by posting questions on one of the many member-to-member question and answer boards. These boards are a platform for you to ask questions, give or get answers, and share information about eBay. Answers are rated according to their helpfulness to other members. Answer Center board topics include:

- **Auction Listings.** On this board, anything related to buying or selling items is fair game. Members ask each other to critique their listings and get advice on how to write more effective descriptions or how to respond to odd or difficult questions from potential bidders.

- **Bidding.** Questions posted here range from queries about the best strategies for bidding to how to retract bids, or, on the sellers' side, how to limit bidding or block certain eBay members from bidding.

- **Checkout.** This is an answer board that all newbies to eBay should definitely visit, as it involves anything regarding payment. All the intricacies of eBay rules regarding prompt payment and shipment of goods are described, and there are numerous questions—with comprehensive answers from multiple members—on how to protect yourself from scams and fraud.

- **eBay Stores.** The place to go if you have any questions about how to set up or run your eBay store. Information here covers the technical aspects of using the eBay Stores tools as well as business advice on how to source merchandise, drive more buyers to your store, or present your products more attractively.

- **Escrow/Insurance.** Here you will find lively discussions on why, when, and how to insure items, whether you are a buyer or seller, and what to do if items get lost or are damaged in transit. Here, as in the Checkout category, a great deal of attention is paid to fraud and scams and how to protect yourself from them.

- **Feedback.** As feedback is one of the most critical aspects of either buying or selling on eBay, this is one of the most active message boards. All participants in the eBay community should read this, as it probes the nuances of this essential (but not quite perfect) system for ensuring the integrity of the eBay marketplace.

- **International Trading.** The entries on this board cover virtually every aspect of international business, from shipping to financial arrangements to currency exchange, translation issues, and cultural differences. As might be expected, fraud is also a hot topic, as many fraud schemes involve international payments or shipments.

- **My eBay.** This board covers mainly technical or procedural questions about accounts and member activity.

- **Packaging & Shipping.** Shipping is a *huge* deal for eBay sellers, and so, not surprisingly, this is one of the most popular boards on the site. Sellers help each other figure out the best shipping carriers for different types of products, how to ensure that items reach the winning bidders intact and on time, and reasonable rates to charge buyers to ship items.

- **PayPal.** Since it is the most-used payment method on eBay, both buyers and sellers are intensely interested in all the ins and outs of this e-payment platform. This board is extremely useful because it provides documentation from actual buyers and sellers about all the things that can go wrong, even with a system as mature as PayPal.

- **Photos/HTML.** This is a largely technical discussion board in which members help each other figure out the best—and cheapest—ways to take and post pictures for auction listings.

- **Policies/User Agreement.** Stating the terms of your sale clearly to the highest bidder—including what kind of payments you will accept, whether you will accept returns if the buyer is not satisfied, or what "shipping and handling" fees will be—is part of being a good and ethical seller. This board is where members answer each other's questions about how to formulate—and enforce—policies for their auctions.

- **Registration.** Here is where eBay members having registration problems—largely administrative—come for answers from other members.

- **Search.** Although supposedly about eBay's search feature, this board seems to be a catch-all for miscellaneous questions about a variety of topics.

- **Technical Issues.** A very popular message board, this one is chock-full of helpful member-to-member advice on everything from browser incompatibilities to problems uploading photographs.

- **Tools.** eBay has tools for sellers—specifically, Turbo Lister and Blackthorne, which can help you create listings and manage sales—and there are several Answer Center boards devoted to how to use them most effectively.

- **Trading Assistant.** Trading Assistants are experienced eBay sellers who sell items for others for a fee. This board is dedicated to questions about the program as well as about individual trading assistants.

- **Trust & Safety.** Anything involving frauds and scams is covered here in depth. All new eBay members—both buyers and sellers—should read this board to understand the sorts of things that can go wrong when dealing with unscrupulous persons in an online marketplace.

- **Discussion Boards.** Unlike the community answer boards, which are organized in a question-and-answer format, the eBay discussion boards are much more freewheeling and expansive and touch upon almost every auction-related subject imaginable. You can join discussions based on general topics or on category-specific topics.

- **Groups.** Even broader in scope are the eBay groups, in which the discussions aren't necessarily focused on eBay but on specific interests like gardening or cooking or archery. Many groups have their own newsletters, events, polls, and even photo albums to draw their virtual communities closer together.

- **Chat Rooms.** If you're tired of the delay between posting a question or comment and getting a reply, you can visit eBay's chat rooms to "talk"—actually, type—in real time with other eBay members about a variety of subjects.

Town Hall Events

Approximately once a month, eBay sponsors a Town Hall event, which is a live, online meeting that gives eBay members a chance to ask questions of senior eBay executives. Open to any registered eBay member, these events last one hour; most of them are general in nature, where any topic related to buying or selling on eBay is fair game. Other events focus on specific events, such as fraud or feedback.

Town Hall events consist of Internet-based live audio "streams" that eBay members can listen to via their computers. After the events, the audio files are archived at the eBay site for anyone to listen to at their convenience.

The Title's the Thing

"*The title is really everything. The one extra I would pay for is a subtitle that further helps to explain what you are selling. It's expensive, but worth it.*"

Zain Naboulsi, BBB member,
eBay PowerSeller, and owner of
Insert Knowledge Here, Mansfield, Texas

Create Compelling Listings

Nine Steps to Auction

O nce you've registered on eBay, know what you're going to sell, and have created a business plan, it's time to set up your first auction. Begin by clicking on the Sell tab on the home page. This will take you to the main Sell page, where you will be asked to describe the item you are selling. The eBay system will walk you through the listing process:

1) **Select a category.** Once you enter a description of the item you want to sell, a list of the most common categories for that type of item will appear. You'll notice a percentage figure on the right-hand side of the screen next to each category. This tells you the percentage of other sellers who chose that category after describing their items using the same words you did. If you type in "drill bit," the category that eBay would recommend would be "Home & Garden > Tools > Power Tools > Drill Bits > Multi-bit Sets," because 50 percent of other sellers who used those keywords also chose that category. If you're selling single bits, that category might not fit. In that case, keep browsing until you find the appropriate category. Click on the category you think is your best fit to continue.

QUICK TIP

Do a Sample Auction

Even if you aren't quite ready to start selling on eBay, do a few sample auctions with inexpensive merchandise to familiarize yourself with the process. You will get comfortable with the mechanics of setting up an auction without taking a significant risk. You may also start to collect positive feedback.

You will be asked if you want to list in a second category. Although this will boost the exposure your item gets, it will also cost you more (how much more will vary, depending on what your item ultimately sells for).

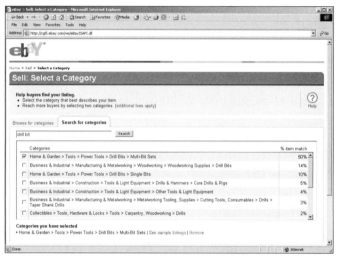

After you enter a description of the item you're selling, you'll see a list of the most common categories for that type of item.

Gallery Photos

A gallery photo is a tiny photo that appears next to your listing title on the Search Results page. This allows buyers to take a quick look at what you are selling without having to actually click through to your listing. Choosing to have one is highly recommended, as many buyers won't even consider looking at an auction that doesn't have a photograph prominently displayed.

2) **Write your title.** The basic listing fee includes a title. Adding a subtitle costs extra—the rates may change, so go to *www.ebay.com* for current eBay pricing.

3) **Upload your photo.** Your Insertion Fee also allows you to post a single photo on your listing. Just enter the image file name, or click on the Browse button to search through your computer and click on the photo's file name in a directory.

4) **Write the item description.** Use powerful, action-oriented language while describing your item completely, clearly, and, above all, honestly. You can choose your text font and size, and whether it is bold, in color, italicized, or contains other special characters. Click on the Preview button to see how your auction listing will appear, and edit it as necessary.

The Right Starting Price

Setting the right starting price for your auction is a combination of art and science. Start the price too low, and you might end up sacrificing your item at a price well below what you paid for it. Set the starting price too high and buyers might be discouraged from bidding. Your best bet for setting an optimal starting price is, as always, research. Using eBay's Completed Listings feature, you can learn what auctions of similar items have started at—and see what they closed at.

5) **Decide whether you want other bells and whistles.** You will be asked to make decisions on a number of other special listings features—things like customized borders and special layouts of photos that could make your listing more attractive to buyers. Keep in mind that each special feature costs you extra—and the fees can add up quickly.

6) **Determine starting price (if any).** Set the price at which the bidding will begin. A starting price of $25.99 means that the first bid must be at least $25.99.

7) **Decide on the duration of your auction.** You can choose between 3 days, 5 days, 7 days, and 10 days.

8) **Specify the payment types you will accept.** This is a critical aspect of setting up your auction. PayPal is the safest option as far as you, the seller, are concerned; you are guaranteed your payment from buyers as soon as they click the payment button. However, in order to attract more bidders, many sellers will accept money orders or personal checks. In the case of the latter payment method, most sellers will hold onto the item until the check has cleared, which can take up to seven business days.

- **PayPal.** The electronic payment method that requires both buyer and seller to be registered with the PayPal service.

- **Money order/cashier's check.** A check from a bank or other financial institution for the amount of the item, made out to the seller.

- **Personal check.** A personal check from the buyer, made out to the seller.

- **Credit cards.** If you already accept credit cards at your brick-and-mortar store, you may also be willing to accept them on eBay.

Accepting Credit Cards

Although PayPal is the payment method of choice for most eBay transactions (see page 66), a number of sellers also accept credit cards. There are a number of advantages to doing this. Many buyers who are new to eBay or online transactions may not have PayPal accounts and may be nervous about trying it, especially if they are new to online financial transactions. Since most people are accustomed to and comfortable with credit cards, offering this as an option can entice more bidders to your auctions.

A second advantage is that all transactions are traceable. If something goes wrong, you can go directly to the credit card company and start the process of querying a transaction. Additionally, you get paid immediately—there's no waiting for a check to arrive in the mail or for PayPal to process the funds and deposit the money in your PayPal account.

Finally, there's the fact that most credit card companies limit the liability of both buyers and sellers—making it an attractive proposition for both parties.

However, these advantages are outweighed by the fact that it costs you money every time you allow a buyer to use a credit card to complete a transaction—and typically, it costs significantly more than using PayPal. If your margins are relatively high—if you sell big-ticket items like PCs, cars, or valuable collectibles—this may be an acceptable cost of doing business. But if you have relatively low margins, accepting a credit card might make the difference between making a profit and merely breaking even or even losing money.

QUICK TIP

Setting the Duration of Your Auction

Although there are all sorts of eBay "experts" who claim to know the best duration to choose for auctions, research shows that, overall, the duration of an auction has little impact on its chances of success. The only way to find out the best window for your type of product or service is to carefully watch what is happening with auctions of similar items and experiment until you arrive at the optimal time to let your item appear before the public.

9) Calculate the shipping costs. In your listing you can specify a flat rate for shipping and handling or provide a link to the eBay Shipping Calculator for buyers to insert their zip code and calculate the cost themselves (see pages 162-163 for more).

Should You Use the Counter?

The eBay counter is a free tool that counts visits to your listing. If you decide to include a counter on your listing—you're asked if you'd like to do this when creating your auction—it will show you the number of times your item has been viewed by potential bidders.

A counter is a good indication of how interested people are in your listing—after all, their visit wouldn't be counted unless they clicked on your title from the Category or Search page. The counter is available in three forms: basic, retro-computer, and

hidden. If you choose one of the first two designs, it will be placed at the bottom of your listing page.

If you expect a large number of visitors to your site, a visible counter will prove to each successive buyer the popularity of the item and motivate them to bid—and bid *more*—for that item themselves. You would hide the counter for the reverse reason: you expect low traffic, but you don't necessarily want visitors to know that. (As the seller of the item, you will, of course, be able to see the number—but no one else will.)

When creating a listing, you'll be given the option of adding a counter.

11

Keys to Compelling Listings

I f an auction takes place on eBay and no one bids, did it actually occur? Technically, it did—after all, you paid the listing fee! But you can't call such an event a success. You have two options at that point: either put the item back in your garage or on your excess inventory shelf, or resubmit it and try again.

It could be, of course, that no one wanted to buy what you had to sell. But odd things sell all the time on eBay. So your problem might be that you just haven't presented your item in the best possible way.

The very best listings can be deceptively simple. They don't necessarily have to have fancy graphics or professional photography (although evidence does suggest that stellar design boosts the value of your auctions). Here's what an effective listing should accomplish:

- **Attract potential bidders.** An effective listing hooks them through the title, the description, the photo, or all three, and gets them to consider bidding on your item.

- **Give them a precise understanding of the item and its condition.** Once they are interested, your job is to provide potential buyers with all the information they need to decide whether they want to proceed with bidding. The more exact you can be about the specifications and

The More Things Change …

Continually browse listings for new ideas. You'd be surprised at the variety of tactics that other sellers use to attract buyers to their auctions. And people are constantly innovating, so it pays to stay on top of evolving trends.

condition of your item, the more informed choices your potential bidders can make. Use effective language and visual evidence to convince buyers that they want what you have to sell.

- **Show them exactly what you're selling.** Posting multiple, clear photos is essential. Include both close-ups and shots from far enough away to show the entire product. You'll have to pay extra for the additional photos, but the resulting bids should amply reward your investment.

- **Persuade them that there is something better or unique about your offer.** You need to distinguish your item from all similar items listed on eBay. Emphasize anything you think gives you an advantage: the rarity or scarcity of the item, that it is brand new, its condition, the quantity available, its size or specifications.

- **Provide them with hope that they can get it at a good price.** There are several ways of doing this. One is to start the bidding at a very low price (99 cents) and allow market forces to run their course. Nothing motivates potential bidders more than the desire to seize a bargain!

- **Convince them that you are reputable and honest and will deliver the goods.** This is critical. Of course, the main source of bidder comfort will be your feedback ratings from previous satisfied buyers, so the longer you are in business—and serving your customers well—the more competitive you will be.

How you present your items, the language you use, even the graphics you choose affect buyers' perceptions of you. Everything in your listing should reflect that you are a trustworthy, attentive-to-details sort of seller who will follow through on commitments and abide by eBay's very strict rules of ethical behavior.

Compelling Titles

Y our title is *the single most important part of your listing.* Think of it as the flag you are waving in front of potential bidders. For many of them, this is the only part of your listing they will see—they will do a search on keywords, or browse through a category, and look at the titles first without bothering to go "deeper" and look at the actual descriptions. The most important thing for you to anticipate, then, is what keywords they are most likely to use when describing what they are looking for.

Say exactly what your item is. Don't try to be overly sales-y in the title—you can do your marketing in the description. Instead, be as clear, straightforward, and precise as possible. Thus: "Rare 1946 black-and-white photographic print by Edward Weston" is infinitely preferable to "Gorgeous rare old photo!"

You are allotted 55 characters for your title. Use as many of them as you can—the more information you can squeeze in, the better. Avoid the use of ALL CAPS or excessive exclamation marks—these just come across as over the top and are as likely to put buyers off as to attract them.

There are three ways to get the attention of eBay shoppers who view your titles on the initial category or search page:

■ **The title itself.** It must stand out from all other listings, yet be full of relevant facts and be absolutely accurate. "24 Hermes d'Orange Verte Perfumed Soaps Save Over 55%!" is a good title, as it tells potential bidders exactly what they will get, as well as listing the benefit—the cost reduction—of the item listed.

■ **A subtitle.** Although there is an additional fee for this, a subtitle adds value. It allows you to provide additional facts about your merchandise that you weren't able to fit into the title itself. It can also provide extra color in the form of descriptive adjectives or active verbs that convey the features and benefits of your product. Thus, having the subtitle "Bluetooth WIFI 4GB Laptop Mini Great Gift Ships in 1 day" to go with the title "New Palm Life Drive Handheld Organizer" provides a considerable amount of additional information to browsers searching for a PDA.

■ **A gallery photo.** Most buyers won't even consider reading through the titles (much less the subtitles) of listings returned by a search unless there is a small, but easily viewable, photo to the side of the title.

QUICK TIP

Spread the Word

Buyers will use the Search feature to locate items of interest. If the keywords they choose aren't in your title or description, they won't find what you have for sale. So don't go out of your way to come up with unusual or unique ways to describe your goods. Instead, make sure you include the words buyers are most likely to use when searching for items like yours.

How do you compose an effective title? The nuances of what you say (and how you present it) depend on the exact type of product you are selling—and the audience you hope to attract—but there are some basic precepts you should keep in mind:

■ **Focus on substance, not hype.** Save the flowery language for your description. Buyers want to know *what* you're selling before they hear about how fantastic, wonderful, and exciting your item is. Tell them up front. Keep your titles clear and concise. Actually, this isn't difficult, as you have so little space!

■ **Anticipate the keywords that potential bidders will search on.** Don't just guess at this. Put yourself in buyers' shoes and experiment. Type in the keywords you would use if searching for an item like yours. Then look at what pops up. Are the results similar to what you are selling? If not, try again. Keep trying keywords until items that are as close to yours as possible appear on the Search Results page. What are the titles that catch your eye? Which ones make you want to click to get more details? Take note of the specific words used—and don't be shy about incorporating them into your own titles.

■ **Include manufacturer, make, model number, size.** Specific identifiers are essential. Women don't just search for "shoes"; they search for "size 9 red designer shoes." Thus, a title that reads "Christian Louboutin Black Prive Red Tip Shoes 40/9.0" with a subtitle "Barely worn designer pumps!" would be vastly more successful than one that doesn't specify maker, size, or color.

Likewise, when searching for a laptop computer, a title that reads "New DELL Inspiron E1405 640m Core Duo 1.6G 1G Ram 160G" with a subtitle "160GB HD - DVD burner - Ultrasharp Truelife LCD - WIFI" is likely to get a lot more clickthroughs than one that reads, "Brand New Laptop!"

■ **Use CAPS, exclamation points, bright colors, or other unusual punctuation judiciously.** Yes, you need to attract attention, but you don't want to come off as one of those shills who stand on city street corners hawking their wares. Overuse of caps can come off as the online equivalent of shouting. Overuse of exclamation marks can actually make you appear less legitimate than if you took a calmer, more subdued approach.

Do:
Engine for 1995 Chrysler Town & Country Minivan MINT CONDITION!

Don't:
FABULOUSENGINE FOR 1995 CHRYSLER TOWN&COUNTRY!!!!!! MUST SEE!!!!

■ **Squeeze as much as you can into 55 characters.** This is very precious space—don't waste it! Use every allotted character if possible. This will often mean that grammar is gone with the wind. That's okay—for perhaps the first time since you learned to write, you won't have to worry about creating complete sentences.

Acronyms

If you use abbreviations—which most people do in titles—don't make up your own! Use standard abbreviations or acronyms. Don't misspell words in order to save space in ways that will appear illiterate rather than clever.

B&W: Black and white

BIN: Buy It Now

EUC: Excellent used condition

FC: Fine condition

G: Good condition

GU: Gently used (item that has been used but shows little wear, accompanied by explanation of wear)

HTF: Hard to find

LTD: Limited edition

MNT: Mint (in perfect condition—a subjective term)

MIB: Mint in box

NBW: Never been worn

NIB: New in box

NR: No reserve price (for an auction-style listing)

NRFB: Never removed from box

NWT: New with tags

NWOT: New without original tags

VHTF: Very hard to find

Brainstorm for a Title

Pick an item you intend to list for auction and use this worksheet to write down every word you associate with it. Don't worry about whether any particular one makes sense or not—just write down your thoughts as they come.

WORDS ASSOCIATED WITH YOUR ITEM

Now, choose the most relevant of these words and string them together in various combinations (trying to get as close to 55 characters, including spaces, as possible without going over) until you come up with a title that will bring in buyers.

	POSSIBLE TITLE	CHARACTER COUNT
1.		
2.		
3.		
4.		
5.		
6.		
7.		
8.		
9.		
10.		

Compelling Descriptions

The meat of encouraging people to bid, bid, bid is in the description. As always, your best guide to good descriptions will be the other listings in your chosen category. Think like a buyer: what would *you* want to know before you would commit to paying a certain amount for an item like this? What questions arise in your mind as you read other, similar listings? What do you wish *they* had included?

Although the precise attributes of what buyers want in a description vary from category to category, here are some basic guidelines to follow when writing your own:

■ **Be absolutely thorough.** This can't be emphasized enough. Buyers have to decide whether to risk bidding on your item (and there always is *some* risk involved). The only thing they have to go on is your description (and the photos—see pages 95-97). Make it easy for them. Tell them everything—and that means *every-thing*—about it, especially any flaws. Is there a dent in one side of the box containing that new silverware set? Explain that (and photograph it). Is there a small discoloration on the inside sleeve of that suit? Disclose it.

This description inspires confidence *because of* its completeness and candor about flaws:

Used Specialized Epic 60 cm Road Bike in color red with black fade. The top tube is 57.5 cm center to center. The frame is carbon fiber with alloy lugs and aluminum fork. All made in USA by Specialized several years ago. Pretty cool road ride actually, but keep in mind that it is used. Although it is very smooth and comfortable, you will need to tune it to take advantage of the nice sprint ability afforded by its early carbon technology. The component group is Campagnolo Mirage 8 speed rear double up front. Complete Campy Mirage group! No mixing. Cranks are Campy Mirage 172.5 mm with 52/39 rings. Frame has very few scuffs and no dents. Comes with an H2O cage that has a crack in the hoop; you may toss it, but I left it on. The computer has cadence, but needs to be recalibrated and/or given a new battery. Please know up front (before you bid) that it might not work; I cannot promise it is in working order. I just didn't have time to mess with it. If you get it working you score a bonus computer with cadence. Overall, this is a good deal for what I am asking and is solid mechanically! The Campy drive wants a lot more miles of fun!

■ **Proper grammar and spelling.** Unlike the title, in which you have to be creative with abbreviations and ignore the need for correct grammar, the description should be carefully written and proofread for typographical errors. If you're not the best speller in the world, make sure you use a spell checker or have someone else read it for you.

Quick Tip

A Second Look

If you're new to creating descriptions and want some feedback on what you've written from more experienced sellers, go to eBay Community Answers (see page 70) and ask if someone there will read it for you. Chances are good that there is an eBay member who will be generous enough to take the time to do so.

Just look at the difference:

Do:

This is a slightly used machine; it works perfectly. I have the user video, but if you don't own a VHS player, you can download the user manual from the Starbucks website. By slightly used, I mean it has been used less than once per month. There are no defects in the machine. You can see in the picture which parts come with the machine. All parts that came with the machine are included except one: the brew head cleaner. There are also items included in the sale that did not come with the machine—namely, the two glasses and the frothing pitcher.

Don't:

This is a usd machine, it works ok. I have video but if you don't own player, you can download from Starbuk's webst onto ur PC. I mean it has been usd 1x a month. Its not broke. Xtra stuff incl.

■ **No ominous language.** Your tone should be friendly and courteous. All too often, descriptions contain admonitions and warnings that sound like barely concealed threats. Statements like "Talk to me before you register a negative comment or I will leave a negative comment for you," or directives in all caps to "READ ALL THE DIRECTIONS CAREFULLY OR DON'T WASTE MY TIME BY BIDDING ON THIS AUCTION" won't exactly inspire confidence in potential buyers. Nothing puts bidders off more than a seller who sounds impatient or even hostile.

■ **Descriptive, yet concise.** Just because you have a full page to write doesn't mean you should run on and on. Your buyers will be put off by excessive verbiage, especially if you are repetitive. As with any kind of writing, you should say what you mean and mean what you say. Be complete, but know when you have made your point. Again, if unsure, ask a friend or another eBay seller to read it over.

Flawless Disclosure of Flaws

The most important thing about your description is that it's honest. If an item has something wrong with it, put that in there. Your reputation is the most important thing— much more important than a few extra dollars earned on one auction.

Christina Cousino, BBB member, eBay PowerSeller, and owner of Foffun's Online Auctions, Napoleon, Ohio

Create the description

Take the time to make sure that your description is complete and that you anticipate any questions buyers may have. Keep in mind that many of the buyers on eBay are experts in their fields; if you sell hardware, for example, you can safely assume that a good percentage of your buyers will be extremely cognizant of hardware manufacturers and quality. If you are imprecise or vague (or, worse yet, make errors), you'll get lots of questions from buyers—and probably lots of missed sales opportunities.

Make sure you cover the following things in your description:

- **Item features.** List all the specifications—color, dimensions, size, weight, quantity, and everything else you can think of that describes the item completely. Don't leave anything out, no matter how minor a point it might seem.

- **Item benefits.** How will purchasing this item make the buyer's life better or easier? Will using the item save them time? Make a task easier? Will buying it from you save them money? Be sure to emphasize the benefits, as well as the features, of what you're selling.

- **Item condition.** This is a critical aspect of your description. Is it new in box (NIB)? Used but still under warranty? Not working? Note any flaws or repairs you (or others) have made very carefully.

- **Answers to common questions.** What material is the item made of? When was it made? What company, artist, designer, or author made it? What country is it from? What is its model and/or make? Does it have a special background or history? Try to anticipate anything that a potential buyer would want to know about your item.

- **Terms and policies.** You must also specify exactly what your policies are with regard to everything about the sale. Do you require the buyer to pay for shipping insurance (many sellers do)? Do you allow for returns? What should a buyer do if not completely satisfied? Anything and everything that a buyer needs to know *before* bidding should be listed in the description. Otherwise, you risk getting negative feedback from winning bidders who feel they weren't adequately informed about all aspects of the listing.

Write Your Listing Description

Pick an item you intend to list for auction and answer the following questions about it. After you've finished filling in this worksheet you will have a list of all the details that should, at minimum, be included in your listing.

QUESTION	ANSWER
What is the item you are selling (be as precise as possible)?	
What is the quantity you are selling in this listing?	
Who made or manufactured it? What is its specific make or model number or other identifying descriptor (such as an ISBN number for books)?	
How old is it (if you don't know, say so)?	
How did you acquire it?	
What color is it?	
What is its height? Width? Weight?	
If apparel or other type of product that has uniform sizes or measurements, what are those sizes/measurements?	
What is the general condition it is in? New? Used but in excellent condition? Gently used? In need of repair?	

continued

QUESTION	ANSWER
What are the specific flaws, problems, malfunctions, repairs made/needed? Be very specific here!	
What are the accessories, instruction manuals, cables, or other items that are included with the item?	
Is there anything unique about this particular item? If so, what?	
Is there anything unique about you, the seller? If so, what?	
Do you have any knowledge of the product's history? If so, what is it?	
Is this product rare or hard to find?	
What kind of payment will you accept? PayPal? Money order? Credit cards? Other?	
How soon after receiving payment will you ship this item?	
How will you ship this item? USPS? FedEx? Other?	
What are your shipping and handling fees?	
Where are you willing to ship to?	
Do you have any restrictions on who can bid on this item?	
Do you require that the buyer pay insurance? What is the cost?	
What is your returns/refunds policy? Under what circumstances will you issue refunds or accept returns?	
What other information should a potential bidder know about you or the item in question? For example, if there is something about the item that a casual reader of the description might not notice—such as a crack in a collectible—you should draw attention to it.	

Compelling Photos

O ther than your title and description, the single most important part of your listing is your photo—or, rather, *photos*. Because experienced eBay sellers report that the more photos you post, the higher the bids will go in your auction.

This is not a book on photography, or a technical manual on how to digitally edit photographs—you can get that information elsewhere. Still, there are some basic things you can do to maximize the impact of your listings.

■ **Buy an excellent digital camera.** Photography is a critical part of your eBay business. A very good camera is a necessary business expense. You'll pay several hundred dollars more for a camera with high enough resolution to take photographs that will appear to best advantage online. If you are serious about your eBay venture, the investment will pay off. Do your research and spend the extra dollars. You'll be glad you did.

■ **Learn how to use it.** Like any piece of sophisticated equipment, digital cameras can be difficult to master. Fortunately, there are classes as well as online tutorials

QUICK TIP

Gallery Photos: A Window into Your Auctions

You shouldn't even consider listing an item without an accompanying gallery photo that will appear next to your title on a specific Category or Search Results page. Most browsers won't even look at listings without gallery photos.

that can walk you through the process of taking the kind of good, clear photographs be required for eBay. As you become more proficient, you'll also want to investigate background and lighting techniques, as well as other, more esoteric aspects of photography.

- **Master your editing software.** This is an important aspect of working with digital photography. Focusing on the subject of the photo, eliminating unnecessary background, lightening or darkening the photo, color correcting—it is actually quite impressive what can be done to a photograph with the touch of a mouse. Again, there are classes in popular programs like Adobe's Elements or Photoshop, numerous free photo editing services available on the Web, and a host of cost-effective intermediary options that fall in between. Remember, however, that you are not trying to hide flaws or misrepresent your items.

- **Photograph your items from every possible angle.** It can be annoying to click on a listing only to find a single photo of an item, taken straight on. For some products, it doesn't matter, of course: if you are selling packaged software, for example, or used DVDs, people don't need to see the front and back of the package. But for many of the items sold on eBay, a 360-degree view is not only desirable, but essential. Be especially vigilant about

QUICK TIP

Use Third-Party Photo Hosting Services

If you intend to use a lot of photos—and you should—you will save a considerable amount of money by using a third-party hosting service. Such services store your item photos online and provide you with easy-to-use tools for selecting the ones you want to include in your eBay listings. Because most third-party vendors offer hosting fees that are significantly lower than eBay's own photo hosting costs, this saves high-volume sellers significant dollars.

photographing any flaws or defects as well as virtues of your item—this will enhance your credibility as a seller and avoid any unpleasant after-sale altercations with buyers.

- **Photograph against a plain background.** Nothing is more frustrating for buyers than trying to pick out the details of your merchandise against a busy background, such as a cluttered table or flowered wallpaper. Make sure there are no visual distractions in the photograph.

Respect Copyright Rules

It is against eBay rules to copy photographs from another listing or to use any material that legally belongs to a third party. This frequently includes promotional photos created by manufacturers and posted on their websites—for example, a photograph of a specific PC or car model. It is the responsibility of the seller to check with the owner of any potentially copyrighted materials to make sure they have the right to use them in a listing.

eBay is committed to protecting the intellectual property rights of third parties and to providing its users with a safe place to trade. To do this, eBay has the Verified Rights Owner (VeRO) Program so that intellectual property owners can easily report listings that infringe their rights. If a property owner—say, a PC manufacturer—sees a photo being misused by an eBay seller and contacts eBay, eBay will send an email to the offending member, asking them to remove the photo. If the buyer does not remove the photo, their membership rights can be suspended indefinitely.

Compelling Graphics

A s you browse eBay listings—which you should be doing constantly—you will see some amazingly sophisticated presentations. Some are as slick as the advertisements you see in glossy magazines. That's no surprise—many serious listers employ professional graphic designers and programmers to achieve maximum visual effect. You have this option, of course. But start with the basic options eBay offers you when designing and customizing your listings.

As you are prompted through the process of creating your listing, eBay will offer you a seemingly endless stream of choices that allow you to distinguish your listing from others. These are called Listing Upgrades, and each one costs you extra. At the end of the process, you will be presented with a "bill" for all the extras you've added. Some of the more popular Listing Upgrades include:

- **Bold.** eBay claims that items with titles in boldface are much more likely to sell than others.

- *Italic*. Like boldface type, this can be used for emphasis.

- Border. This upgrade puts a border around your listing.

QUICK TIP

No Buyer's Remorse

If you go a little wild on special features while you're creating your listing and are shocked at the end by how much it will cost you, don't worry—at just about every opportunity, eBay lets you preview what your listing will look like and gives you the opportunity to go back and edit your choices.

- **Highlight.** This option highlights your listing with a colored band of your choosing.

- **Listing Designer**. This gives you dozens of different design templates to choose from (more are added regularly) that can improve the appeal of your listing. Of course, other sellers have access to these same templates, but they are a cost-effective way of presenting a professional appearance without learning HTML, paying for custom design work, or acquiring design templates from third-party vendors.

Each of the templates that eBay offers (technically, they are called "themes") automatically adds background color, pictures, and other design features to your basic description. A "Books" theme will showcase your description as if it were the cover of a book; a "Business Industrial" theme has a faux wooden border.

You will also be presented with some basic layout choices, such as how to place your photos in relation to your text, whether your text is centered or not, and other graphic options. At each stage you can preview your selection to see how it looks until you find something that you like.

Third-Party Listing Design Services

One of the most fascinating things about the eBay phenomenon is that it has spawned a massive spin-off industry of small (and, increasingly, not-so-small) companies that offer specialized products and services to support eBay sellers. There is a broad range of help you can call upon when designing your listings. This help ranges from services offered by professional designers who can create a unique design for individual listings or templates for you to use over and over again, to companies that will sell you sophisticated templates that you can customize yourself. Some templates are even available on the Web for free, or for an extraordinarily low (or voluntary) contribution! Once you get serious about your eBay selling, you will almost certainly want to check out your design alternatives.

The eBay Solutions Directory

The number of software programs available to help you more efficiently manage your auctions grows every week. Some are available from eBay itself; others come from third-party vendors. To help you find a software solution that's right for you, go to the Solutions Directory (*www. solutions.ebay.com*), where you can browse a number of categories or search based on keywords. For example, if you are looking for ways to better manage your item photographs, you could browse through the offerings in the Photo Hosting & Management category or do a search using "photo management," and a list of available products—both from eBay and from independent software providers—will display.

Listing Upgrades

D on't just assume that creating an attractive and comprehensive listing means you will be overrun with visitors to your auction page—and huge numbers of bidders. You will also need to drive buyers to your site using other marketing techniques. eBay provides you with a number of options that will help you do that. Called Listing Upgrades, these include everything from special fonts such as boldface and italics to being featured on eBay's home page. Each Listing Upgrade costs money and the fees can add up, especially if you are listing dozens or even hundreds of items, as many PowerSellers do.

Splurge on "Featured Items" placement

If you pay for this upgrade, your item will be displayed in the Featured Items section of its category—actually, subcategory, as your first click on any one category will bring up a list of subcategories rather than auction items themselves. For example, if sellers click on the Antiques category, they will have to click further—on, say, "Rugs, Carpets"—to get to the Featured Items. Featured Items (photo, title and sub-title, and auction details, but no description) are displayed prominently *before* the regular auction listings. If you choose this option, your item will also be displayed in its usual spot within the Category or Search Results pages.

Upgrade further to "Featured Plus!"

When you perform a search using keywords—whether within a particular category or throughout the entire eBay

Join SquareTrade

On eBay, credibility is everything. Anything you can do to promote the fact that you are an honest and reputable seller who will treat buyers fairly will help you get more bidders—as well as increase the cash that your auctions generate. Displaying the SquareTrade logo (see page 102) is a good way to convince would-be buyers that you are on the up-and-up.

site—the search results can be organized by the listing end date, price, or other options. You can choose how you'd like to organize the results by clicking on the appropriate pull-down menu at the top of the page and making a selection there. You'll see 50 results per page. Your Featured Plus! item will appear at the *top* of the page it naturally falls on in the Search Results list.

If a buyer chooses to view listings by end date, your featured item would not move up through the other items, but would appear where it ordinarily would, given its designated end date. However, your listing would also be prominently displayed at the top of that same page. Featured Plus! is only available to sellers with a feedback rating of 10 or more.

Offer Gift Services

If you think your item would make a good gift—especially around the holiday season—you can pay extra to feature it in that way. When you purchase the Gift Services listing upgrade, a gift icon will appear next to your listing. You then have the option of offering buyers one or more of three gift services:

- Gift wrap/gift card

- Express shipping

- Ship to gift recipient (rather than to buyer)

If you decide to offer any of these services, you should include all details as well as extra charges in your item description.

Promote your listing in the Gallery

Each category or search results page has a Gallery link at the top. If you pay extra, the photo of your item will be featured, along with your title and (if you have one) subtitle, when buyers click on that. In effect, they are browsing by image rather than text. If your item has a strong visual component, it could make sense to upgrade to this listing feature.

Participate in the Gallery

If you participate in a category in which the appearance of the item matters significantly —for example, art, furniture, or apparel—you should seriously consider investing in the Gallery feature, as this is the first thing that will catch would-be buyers' eyes as they browse through a category or view the results of a keyword search.

Go further by being "Gallery Featured"

If you choose this promotional option, a photo of your item (plus title and subtitle) will appear *above* the general picture gallery.

Snag a spot on eBay's home page

Your listing can actually appear on the eBay home page. Fees vary according to the type of auction and the number of items in your listing. Your listing will be displayed in eBay's Featured Items page and will rotate with other items on eBay's home page in the special Featured section.

You need a feedback score of at least 10 in order to use Home Page Featured. Home Page Featured cannot be used for:

- Adult listings

- Listings for services or the sale of information

- Promotional or advertising listings

- Listings for novelty items of questionable taste

- Auction utility software

- Listings that do not offer a genuine auction by eBay listing policies

- Prohibited, questionable, and infringing items

The SquareTrade Seal

Like the Good Housekeeping Seal of Approval, the Square-Trade Seal is one way for sellers to show bidders that they are committed to high selling standards and have had their identities verified by a third party.

To get the SquareTrade Seal, sellers need to go to Square-Trade's website at *www.squaretrade.com* (eBay does not own SquareTrade—it's an independent third party), apply for the seal, and pay a monthly fee should their application be accepted. To retain a SquareTrade Seal, sellers must:

- Agree to participate in SquareTrade's dispute resolution process should a problem arise

- Have their identity verified by SquareTrade

- Commit to SquareTrade's standards for online selling

The SquareTrade Dispute Resolution Process

If for any reason buyers are unhappy with the results of an auction of a seller displaying the SquareTrade Seal, they can file a complaint and the SquareTrade seller is obliged to respond. Sellers can also file claims against buyers, and SquareTrade will facilitate the negotiations between them. Square-Trade also guarantees buyers refunds on fraudulent transactions up to $250 for any listings that display a legitimate SquareTrade Seal.

Step 1: File a case. On the SquareTrade website, buyers and sellers alike may fill out an online form that lets them specify the problem as well as suggest solutions.

Step 2: SquareTrade notifies the other party. SquareTrade lets the other party know that a case has been filed and asks them to respond.

Step 3: The parties discuss their issues directly. In a process called "direct negotiation," once both parties are aware of the issues, they are first asked to try to reach a solution themselves. Their "negotiations" take place online, using a Web-based communication tool to avoid email exchanges that get out of control or the kind of angry shouting matches that can occur by telephone.

Step 4: Mediation. If the buyer and seller cannot come to an agreement, they can request that SquareTrade provide a mediator to try to develop a fair, mutually agreeable solution. It's important to understand that the mediators' role is to facilitate positive, solution-oriented discussion between the parties, but *not* to act as a judge. They will only recommend a resolution if the parties request it, but this recommendation is not binding.

Step 5: The case is resolved—or not. If all goes well, both buyer and seller walk away from the negotiating table satisfied that a fair resolution has been reached. There is always the chance, however, that no agreement is possible—SquareTrade cannot guarantee this, it can only structure the process to facilitate a solution.

Dollars and Sense

"*Understand all your costs before listing items on eBay. Figure out your break-even point. Know that there will be a listing fee, and then a 'Value Fee' when your item sells. If your buyer pays through PayPal, that's another cost. And don't forget shipping, which can be quite expensive. So if you've bought something for $15 and sell it for $20 on eBay, you've actually lost money. Think this through ahead of time.*"

Robert Britton, BBB member,
eBay PowerSeller, and owner of Sterling Trading,
Whitmore Lake, Michigan

Pricing *and* Profits

Cost of Goods Sold

I f you're serious about starting a *business* on eBay, not just clearing some items out of your garage, then you must spend time figuring out how much you will need to charge for your items in order to make a profit. In an auction setting such as the eBay marketplace, you may feel that you have little or no control over pricing, so you don't need to pay attention to setting prices. But this isn't entirely true. You have control over pricing through:

- **The choice of merchandise you sell.** You can choose to sell only those items that command higher prices or are unique and have less competitive pricing pressure.

- **Whether or not you use fixed-price sales instead of, or in addition to, auctions.** You can list an actual price and only offer an item to buyers at that price.

- **Whether you place reserve prices on your auction items or set a higher starting bid.** This ensures that you don't sell items for less than the amount you need to cover your costs.

- **How much you spend to run your business**. You can lower your costs of doing business, thus making it possible to sell your goods at lower prices and still make money.

Moreover, if you already sell your merchandise through traditional brick-and-mortar channels such as retail stores, or through distributors, you may already have prices set for your products. You may think that you can charge the same amount once you start doing business on eBay.

But eBay is a different environment from the brick-and-mortar world. If you run the only hardware store in your town, you can charge a premium price for power drills, since you're providing convenience to your customers as well as a product. But in eBay, all the other sellers of power drills are equally available, so your prices must be more competitive.

Additionally, many competitors in the eBay world keep their cost of doing business exceptionally low by working from home or from areas with low rental costs, by employing family members, or by paying themselves little or no money. This also creates downward pressure on the prices you can set in the eBay marketplace.

So you have to figure out how much the items you're interested in selling can be sold for on eBay and then determine whether such prices will enable you to make a profit—that is, to cover all the costs of doing business with money to spare.

QUICK TIP

Time Is Money

Many, if not most, eBay sellers forget to value their own time when determining whether they're making a profit. When calculating prices and profits on your merchandise, be certain you are building in an income for yourself, as well.

Understand your business expenses

As in any business, the key to setting prices—and making money—on eBay is to sell your products for more money than your costs. But to do so, you have to understand what affects your "costs."

A novice entrepreneur may think, "I bought this product for $100 and sold it for $125, so I've made money." But that $100 is only one component of your expenses—it's the *cost of goods sold*. To determine whether you're really making money on the sale, you have to consider your other costs as well.

In an eBay business, your total costs include:

- Cost of goods sold (see pages 108-109)

- Basic operational expenses (see pages 114-121)

- Expenses associated with running an e-commerce (online sales) business (see page 122)

- eBay specific expenses (see pages 123-126)

- Your time

QUICK TIP

Purchase for Profits

Reducing the cost of goods sold is perhaps the most critical key to making a profit on eBay. You will need to look continually for new sources of inventory to sell or for raw materials to use in the manufacture of your products.

Cost of goods sold (COGS)

How much do you have to pay to get the items you sell online? The cost to acquire the items you sell on eBay is going to dramatically affect how much you can afford to charge and whether or not you'll make a profit. Your cost of goods sold—also referred to as COGS—is your most basic expense.

If you are reselling finished products, then your cost of goods sold is how much you had to pay to buy those products. For instance, if you are selling jewelry you're buying from a jewelry manufacturer, the cost of goods sold is the price you pay for the jewelry. If you are making a product yourself, then your COGS is how much it cost you to make the product (in terms of raw materials and direct labor costs). Thus, if you're making jewelry yourself, your cost of goods sold would include the cost of the materials you use to make the jewelry you sell.

For most eBay entrepreneurs, COGS is the most critical expense. In the online world, prices are very competitive, so you have to be especially adept at keeping your COGS low. Finding a continuing supply of competitively priced quality goods is one of the biggest challenges of running an eBay or other online auction business. You will have a distinct advantage on eBay if you are an exceptionally good buyer or if you manufacture unique items and are able to carefully manage production costs.

eBay COGS

Use the following worksheets to help you identify *at least* five different sources and suppliers of goods you can sell on eBay. Compare prices between different types of sources and from a number of different suppliers of each type. This will give you a more realistic idea of how much your cost of goods sold will be.

Use the first worksheet if you plan to resell finished goods, the second if your goal is to take your existing brick-and-mortar store online, and the third if you expect to manufacture products for sale (because even if you're creating your own products, you'll have to find sources and suppliers for the materials you'll need to make what you sell).

Cost of Goods Sold: Buying for Resale

TYPE OF SOURCE	TYPES OF GOODS	PRICE
Original Manufacturers		
Source 1:		
Source 2:		
Source 3:		
Distributors/wholesalers		
Source 1:		
Source 2:		
Source 3:		
Flea markets/auctions		
Source 1:		
Source 2:		
Source 3:		
Private parties (garage sales, classified ads, and so on)		
Source 1:		
Source 2:		
Source 3:		
Overstock/past season from retailers		
Source 1:		
Source 2:		
Source 3:		
Other eBay sellers		
Source 1:		
Source 2:		
Source 3:		
Other		
Source 1:		
Source 2:		
Source 3:		

Cost of Goods Sold: Taking an Existing Business Online

TYPE OF SOURCE	TYPES OF GOODS	PRICE
Original manufacturer, distributor/wholesaler		
Source 1:		
Source 2:		
Source 3:		
New inventory purchased only for online sales		
Source 1:		
Source 2:		
Source 3:		
Overstock/past season's merchandise from other retailers		
Source 1:		
Source 2:		
Source 3:		
Overstock/past season's merchandise from own inventory		
New, in-stock inventory		
Used products from customers		
Other		
Source 1:		
Source 2:		
Source 3:		

Cost of Goods Sold: Creating Products for Sale

TYPE OF SOURCE	TYPES OF GOODS	PRICE
Raw material #1		
Source 1:		
Source 2:		
Source 3:		
Raw material #2		
Source 1:		
Source 2:		
Source 3:		
Raw material #3		
Source 1:		
Source 2:		
Source 3:		
Raw material #4		
Source 1:		
Source 2:		
Source 3:		
Other		
Source 1:		
Source 2:		
Source 3:		

Drop Shipping: Lucrative or Risky Business?

There are many businesses that want to capitalize on the desire of eBay sellers to keep their COGS as low as possible. Once you start selling on eBay, you are sure to start getting emails from businesses that call themselves "drop shippers" or that offer to put you in touch with drop shippers.

Drop shipping is a technique used by a retailer—either an online seller or the publisher of a traditional mail-order catalogue—that does not keep any products in stock, but instead takes customer orders and forwards them to a wholesaler, which ships the ordered goods directly to the customer. The retailer collects the money from the customer, pays the wholesaler its share, and—theoretically at least—gets to keep the difference between the wholesale price and the amount the customer pays.

When it works, it can work very well indeed. Some very successful eBay PowerSellers do all their business via drop shipping and turn a healthy profit.

But there are also risks to drop shipping. Some of them are the legitimate risks of doing business: you could auction off an item on eBay, only to end up with a winning bid that is less than the wholesale price. Since you're contractually obligated to honor the auction, you've lost money on the sale.

Another risk is that the wholesaler could run out of the product you are selling. Say you list an auction for a certain brand and model of lawnmower, but after the auction closes, you discover that that item is back ordered at the wholesale level. This means that *your* customer might have to wait weeks, or even months, to get the lawnmower in hand. This reflects badly on you and will probably hurt your eBay feedback rating.

Then there are the actual scams surrounding drop shipping. The most common one involves purchasing a list of drop shippers that is supposed to lead you to a steady and profitable source of goods. But the list turns out to be either full of bogus names or contains businesses that are not wholesalers but other retailers who mark up their merchandise as well as charging exorbitant fees for their shipping services, thus making it difficult—if not impossible—for you to earn a decent profit. Unfortunately, many eBay sellers, hungry for a reliable and cheap source of marketable goods, frequently fall for drop shipping scams.

Your best protection against drop shipping scams is a two-step process: first, before handing over any money for any drop ship wholesaler list, check with the BBB at *www.bbb.org*. The BBB has an easy-to-use database with more than three million Reliability Reports on all types of businesses. Also ask for at least three or four references, and call them up. If they turn out to be legitimate businesses with solid eBay feedback ratings, you've reduced the risk of buying the list considerably.

The second action to take is to do the math. Don't just accept a drop shipper's word that selling a certain item will be profitable for you—run the numbers and be sure to add up *all* fees—eBay's as well as the drop shipper's. And check the Internet for comparable prices on the item the "wholesaler" is offering you. If they are suspiciously close to the retail price offered by other online sellers, you may be getting scammed.

Operational Costs

Y our operational costs are those expenses that you incur as a result of doing your day-to-day business. These fall into a number of categories, including:

- Workspace
- Utilities
- Labor
- Transportation
- Education and training
- Office supplies
- Insurance
- Professional services
- Packing and shipping
- Other operating expenses

QUICK TIP

Lean, Not Mean

The eBay marketplace is intensely competitive, keeping sale prices low. That means you must keep the costs of running your business low if you want to make a reasonable profit. Watching your ongoing, day-to-day expenses is critical to survival and success.

Workspace

If you are starting your eBay business from your home, you may not incur any immediate additional workspace costs. Or the costs may be very minor, such as buying a desk, a table for processing orders, or a shelving system for the garage to store inventory. Other eBay businesses may have significant workspace costs. If you are dealing with large or heavy items or industrial equipment, you may need a warehouse and/or shipping area. If you are manufacturing products, you may need other commercial property.

Even with a relatively small eBay business, you may find that you need to rent an additional storage unit at some point. Or you may choose not to work out of your home and decide to rent an office space.

When considering workspace costs, include office, warehouse/storage, shipping, and manufacturing. If you have vehicles for your online business, include the cost of garaging those vehicles, if any.

Utilities

Your monthly overhead will also include the cost of your utilities—electricity, heating, air conditioning, natural gas. If you are working from home for the first time, you're likely to see a fairly substantial rise in your monthly bills. If you are renting space, you must factor these costs into your monthly expenses. Expect them to rise annually.

You should also include your telecommunications costs as a basic utility. In addition to your basic phone expense, you're likely to have expenses for a PDA or other mobile device and text messaging services, along with your Internet access charges. If you are manufacturing products, your utility costs could be substantial.

Separate Shipping from Transportation

This category is for *your* transportation and travel expenses. Keep your *shipping expenses* separate so you can quickly see whether you are recapturing your shipping costs, either by adding these costs onto your basic cost of goods sold or by charging customers enough to cover shipping expenses.

Labor

If you hire employees—whether full- or part-time, permanent or temporary—you will have salaries to pay, as well as your share of social security, payroll taxes, and, potentially, health insurance expenses.

Many small businesspeople fail to hire the help they need to enable their businesses to grow. When you first start your eBay business, you're likely to do most of the tasks yourself. But as your business grows, you may find it makes more sense, and results in more profit, if you hire people to help you. If you personally are the creator of your products (perhaps you design wearable art clothing), you may find you want someone to help you with the administrative functions of your business and to help manage your auctions so that you have more time to work on creating your designs. Or, if you find a lot of your valuable time is taken up packing and shipping items you've sold, you may decide you need the assistance of a part-time shipping clerk. You may not need help all year round. Many businesses are seasonal—especially busy, for instance, during the holiday season.

Then there's the cost of your own labor. As in any business, it takes a while before a new business starts to make a profit. So it's likely that you'll probably work for free at first, while you launch your business and get used to the eBay way of doing business. But that is not sustainable over the long term. Try to estimate how much your time is worth and how much you need to earn to make sure your eBay business is viable over the long term.

Transportation

Your transportation costs will vary greatly depending on what types of products you sell and how you source them. If, for instance, you go to flea markets to find merchandise, you're likely to have significant (and ever-rising) costs for gasoline and auto expenses. If you fly to Asia to find merchandise, you might incur substantial travel expenses. On the other hand, your transportation expenses might be limited to an occasional trip to the post office or office supply store, in which cases, these costs would be minimal.

Education and training

Every good businessperson keeps their knowledge and skills up to date. This means continual education and training. Such education may be related to the type of goods you sell and/or how to run an online e-commerce business. As you consider your education and training expenses, include costs such as taking classes, attending conferences or trade shows (including your travel expenses), subscriptions to magazines, journals, or online content, memberships in trade organizations, and purchase of books.

Office supplies

Office supplies are an important, but often overlooked, ongoing expense. You cannot run a business without them. They include everything from paper and printer supplies to pens and paper, staples, and the all-important packing and shipping supplies—everything you need to keep your business humming.

Insurance

Although this is an expense you might consider expendable, you should not be without adequate insurance. What if you get burglarized? What if there's a fire? Or a supplier delivering goods trips and falls on your pavement? Any of these events could have a devastating impact on your business. You might consider buying any or all of these types of insurance:

- **Fire insurance.** Covers cost of premises and contents in case of destruction or damage by fire.

- **Contents insurance.** Covers specified contents, generally in case of theft.

Keep on Learning

The world of eBay changes frequently, so you'll improve your chances of success by continually improving your skills and staying on top of new developments. eBay offers a number of ways to improve your knowledge and skills, most of them free and online. To find listings, go to the Community tab on the eBay home page, look for Education, and check out Workshops, the Learning Center (including eBay University), Mentoring Groups, and more.

- **Business interruption insurance.** Protects you in case something happens that prevents you from running business as usual, particularly useful for protection in the case of major emergencies.

- **General liability insurance.** Essential for protecting yourself against damage claims for injury or destruction to anyone or anything on your premises, especially if you have foot traffic or visits from customers, suppliers, or business partners.

- **Additional vehicle insurance.** If, as will be likely, you use your car for business purposes, you should get your car insured for business use.

- **Product liability insurance.** This protects you if a buyer sues you because your product harmed them in some way or didn't perform up to your claims.

Quick Tip

An Ounce of Prevention ...

It's easier—and cheaper—to stay out of trouble than to deal with serious problems after they arise. A one-hour consultation with an attorney or accountant to help you set up your business correctly can prevent headaches later.

Professional services

When you are in business, you will need assistance from certain key professionals— attorneys, accountants, graphic designers, and so forth. These may be ongoing, monthly expenses (hiring a bookkeeper, for example) or, more likely, expenses, such as a once-a-year consultation with a tax accountant.

- **Bookkeeping/accounting.** When you start out, you may well keep your own accounts, using a spreadsheet like Microsoft's Excel. As you grow, however, you may want to get advice from an accountant or even engage one to take over all bookkeeping chores for you.

- **Legal.** It is always a good idea to work with a lawyer when you first set up a business, to help you understand the basics of operating a company in your state, liability issues, employment law if you have employees, and so on. You will also need an attorney's advice occasionally during the normal course of business.

- **Consulting.** You may also decide you'd like to get advice from an expert. Whether that's someone from the eBay community, or an independent management consultant, or even someone expert in your particular subject area, you should set aside some money to cover this kind of professional service.

- **Graphic designers.** You want to present a professional image to the world, so you may choose to seek the assistance of a designer. Some of the tasks you may use them for include designing marketing materials, a logo, and packaging.

Packing and shipping

Shipping is one of the largest expenses of running an eBay business. Happily, you can pass on most, if not all, of the actual shipping expenses to your customers (it's best to specify in the auction listing itself what those charges will be). However, you will also need packing supplies—sometimes quite specialized, especially if you sell delicate or oddly shaped objects—and containers. You can recoup some of these expenses by including a "handling" fee in your shipping price, but be warned: the eBay community frowns on excessive shipping and handling costs—especially when they are not disclosed ahead of time. (For more information on packing and shipping, see pages 161-170.)

Leasing Your Equipment

An alternative to paying upfront for your capital equipment is to lease it—that is, to pay a monthly fee to a vendor or leasing company for the privilege of using it for a particular length of time. Depending on the exact terms of the lease, you may have the option to buy the equipment at the end of the specified period, or turn the equipment in and get new, updated equipment and begin the leasing process all over again.

One of the major advantages to leasing is that it reduces your total upfront financial investment. For a monthly fee, you can get what you need to start selling. If you need to purchase very expensive equipment, leasing is usually an attractive option. That's particularly true if you need vehicles or heavy industrial equipment. But many of the costs of starting an eBay business do not generally justify leasing equipment. It doesn't make much sense to lease one computer or one camera.

Other operating expenses

You'll almost certainly have other expenses that are either unique to the type of products/services you sell or that will come up from time to time. Try to project those expenses if you have a reasonable expectation of what they are. Or, add a miscellaneous line to your annual budget to account for some unexpected expenses. When considering other operating expenses, include:

- **Inventory storage.** You may be able to store your inventory in your home—in the basement, the garage, or even on the shelves of your office. But your items might be bulky or large enough to warrant renting warehouse or other storage space.

- **Returns/breakage and inventory "shrinkage."** This expense also varies based on what you sell. If you sell delicate or breakable items, you can almost certainly expect that there will be some breakage—either on your side or in transit to the buyer. It's best to build in a percentage of your overall cost of goods sold that you'll need to write off for this reason. Likewise, even if you are the most careful of record keepers and are extremely vigilant about the items you sell, you may want to include estimates of the costs arising from the fact that some percentage of your inventory will mysteriously disappear (the accepted term is "inventory shrinkage").

- **Uncollected accounts payable.** Unfortunately, on eBay, as in traditional brick-and-mortar stores, you will have deadbeats who write bad checks, forge money orders, or just plain refuse to pay. You should include in your cost estimates the fact that this is likely to happen at some point or another.

- **Equipment leasing expenditures.** If you decide to take this route rather than paying upfront for your PCs, printers, fax machines, and other equipment, you need to account for the cost in your monthly expense estimates.

- **Other equipment.** Depending on the type of eBay business you plan on starting, you may need other equipment. You might require a trailer in which to transport goods, a soldering iron, or a mannequin to model outfits.

- **Finance charges.** You may have to spend money to purchase inventory or material many months before you are able to sell your products. To finance those expenditures, you may have to put charges on your credit card or get a line of credit from a bank. Either way, it's likely you'll incur finance charges. Plan for those in your projections.

Basic Operational Expenses

Use this worksheet to estimate the basic operational expenses for your eBay business. When your business has been in operation for a few months, you can compare the estimated and actual totals.

COST	ESTIMATED MONTHLY	ACTUAL MONTHLY
Workspace		
Utilities		
Labor		
Transportation		
Education and training		
Office supplies		
Insurance		
Professional services		
Packing and shipping		
Other operating expenses		
TOTAL		

Online Business Costs

Whether you're doing business on eBay or in any other online marketplace, you'll be engaged in running a technology-based company. As such, your business requires an investment in *basic* technology and online equipment and services.

This can be fairly simple. After all, eBay was designed with non-technology entrepreneurs in mind, so you can get up and running on eBay with only a minor amount of technological equipment. Moreover, there's an army of third-party providers who will take over or automate many of the functions you'll need, reducing your upfront expenses in equipment (although that may raise your ongoing costs, either monthly costs or costs of each sale).

But you can't avoid the basic costs of running an online company. These include:

■ **Computer(s).** You can't do business without a computer, either a desktop or laptop, depending on how mobile you intend to be. You'll eventually want a backup computer, even for a relatively small eBay business, just in case the first one is out of commission.

■ **High-speed Internet connection.** This is your lifeline to the marketplace.

■ **Printer(s).** You'll need to print copies of online transactions for your records, create shipping labels, and perform other tasks that require hard copies of documents.

■ **Telephone/cell phone.** You will need at least one, and possibly more, telephones. You'll probably want to get a cell phone to be able to answer customer inquiries even when you're away from your desk, as eBay is a 24/7 market.

■ **Digital camera.** eBay customers depend on photos; even before they open a detailed listing of a product, they'll typically see a photo. You'll need fairly high-quality digital photos for all the products you sell.

■ **Photo software.** You don't want to change or misrepresent the items you're selling, but you often have to improve the quality of photos (for instance, lighting exposure), and at least some basic photo manipulation software is necessary.

■ **Technical support.** Eventually, you're going to run into technical problems and need some professional help. This might be something as simple as one-time assistance setting up a wireless connection throughout your home, or something such as ongoing technical assistance for maintaining a network of computers. But sooner or later, you're going to need assistance that costs money, and you should consider those expenses in your overall technology budget.

Optional technology expenses:

■ **PDA/mobile email.** You may well want an electronic device so that you can monitor your auctions when you're away from your desk.

■ **Fax machine.** You may also want a fax machine to better communicate with some customers.

■ **VoIP.** If you're going to be having many phone conversations with your buyers or suppliers, especially if you are doing business internationally, consider using a "VoIP," or Voice over Internet Protocol, service. This is phone service that is channeled through the Internet and tends to be considerably less expensive than traditional land line phone service. eBay owns one such VoIP service, Skype, and you can connect a link to that service to your listings.

eBay Fees

e Bay makes money from the fees it charges to sellers—both from every transaction and for the services it offers. One of the most important things you can do as you start your eBay business is to know what it will take to make a profit given those fees. Once you understand the eBay fee structure, there are a number of strategies you can employ to try and achieve the highest possible profit margin for your goods.

When considering eBay fees, it's best to think about those that are mandatory and those that are optional. Even if you find that many of the optional items are absolutely essential to your business, they are not required by eBay, so you have more control over how much to spend on such services.

eBay changes its fee structure from time to time, so it's best to visit the site and acquaint yourself with eBay fees before you start doing business—and to review those options and fees at least a couple times a year thereafter.

QUICK TIP

Talk to Other Members

Although eBay members can be very protective of their business secrets, this usually applies only within their particular category. Try posting any questions you have about eBay fees or calculating other business expenses on one of the general eBay message boards, and you'll get lots of helpful answers.

Fee Circumvention

One of the biggest no-nos on eBay is something called "fee circumvention." It happens when a seller offers would-be buyers a chance to buy an item "off line," or outside eBay. The reason for this ban is obvious: eBay makes most of its money from final sales fees. If there is no sale, they don't get that money.

Some sellers try to be more subtle than simply making a bold offer to buyers. They make offers in their listing to sell "extras" after the eBay sale. This happens most frequently with items that have many accessories and components, like computers or vehicles. A seller might offer to "upgrade" a buyer to a PC with more power or memory—and because that upgrade would happen outside eBay, eBay wouldn't get its cut.

eBay forbids anything that even faintly resembles fee circumvention and will remove your auctions if it detects that you are violating this policy.

Mandatory eBay fees

■ **Insertion Fee.** There is a basic mandatory fee for listing your item on eBay, whether or not it sells. This fee will vary depending on the specific type of listing and services you choose. For example, a Buy It Now auction costs more than a standard auction, and a 10-day auction costs more than a 5- or 7-day auction (see below).

■ **Final Value Fee.** This is a fee that eBay takes, based on a percentage of how much your item finally sells for. It can be substantial, depending on the value of the items you are selling.

Optional eBay fees

■ **Listing Appearance Fees.** Depending on how enticing—or comprehensive—you want your listing to be, you will pay more. When you add a subtitle, feature a photo of your item on the Search Results page, or include more than one photo of what you're selling, expect your basic listing fee to inch up.

■ **Reserve Price Auction Fee.** You will pay more if you decide to set a reserve for your auction (see page 139).

■ **Buy It Now Fee.** The same is true if you select the Buy It Now option (see page 146).

■ **Scheduled Listing Fee.** This feature allows you to set the precise time when your auction will be listed ahead of time, on a schedule predetermined by you. If you have a lot of items to list—especially if they are similar—this could well be worth the money.

■ **10-Day Auction Fee.** Most auctions last for five or seven days. Fees for those types of auctions are included in the basic Insertion Fee. But if you decide that you would benefit by stretching out the duration of the auction—in effect, putting your item in front of the public for a longer period of time—you will pay for that privilege.

- **Gift Services Fee.** This is the eBay charge for offering your customers the option of having your item wrapped and sent to a third-party address rather than their address (which is otherwise a requirement).

- **Home Page Featured Fee.** This is what you pay—and it is a considerable amount—to have your auction featured on the eBay home page. Note that your item is not fixed there—it is simply rotated along with other Featured Items for a certain period of time.

- **PayPal Fee.** If you decide to accept payment via PayPal, you will have to pay a transaction fee every time a buyer chooses this payment option. Though this is the most convenient way to receive payment—and the one most favored by buyers—the fees can add up depending on the volume of business you do.

When you first launch your eBay business, you will not have a realistic idea of which of the optional eBay services you'll want to use—although you will certainly want to use some of them. Over time, and by participating in eBay community discussion forums, you will get a feel for which services work best for you in increasing the number of sales and the dollar amount at which you make sales. That will help you get a more realistic sense of whether your sales are actually profitable.

Quick Tip

Keep Track of Your Fees

Before you go "feature happy," add up how much all the various fees are going to cost you and make sure that you will still turn an acceptable profit on your sales. Otherwise, it doesn't matter how great your listing looks—you're not succeeding in your primary goal.

eBay Fees

Use this worksheet to calculate how much you'll spend on eBay fees each month. Go to *www.ebay.com* for the latest information on fees, then multiply each fee you'll pay by the number of items you think you'll sell each month. When your business has been in operation for a few months, you can compare the estimated and actual totals.

FEE	ESTIMATED	ACTUAL
Insertion Fee		
Final Value Fee		
Listing Appearance Fee		
Reserve Price Auction Fee		
Buy It Now Fee		
Scheduled Listing Fee		
10-Day Auction Fee		
Gift Services Fee		
Home Page Featured Fee		
PayPal Fee		
Total		

How Much to Charge

I n classic economic theory, a marketplace such as eBay should establish the optimum price for every product. After all, buyers and sellers come together in a very open environment, where all can easily see competitors and sources. And, to a large extent, this is true. It's much more difficult to inflate prices in an eBay environment than in a regular retail situation, where buyers may have fewer choices and demand may be affected by local conditions, events, or personal relationships. As a result, you have less ability to manage your pricing on eBay than you would in other sales environments.

So, knowing your costs of doing business, you need to figure out whether you can make a comfortable profit on eBay selling the products you intend to sell or whether you must readjust your business plan—either changing the products you intend to sell or changing how you intend to run your business.

Completed Listings

eBay provides the single best source of information about what kind of cash you can expect from selling your items on eBay: a record of what similar items have sold for in the recent past.

Called "Completed Listings," this is one of the most powerful tools available for helping you create and execute your business plan. As part of the eBay community, you have free access to auction data from the last seven days. Find it by clicking on Advanced Search, entering keywords for the items whose prices you'd like to research, and checking the "Completed

Value-Density Ratio

The value-density ratio is the pro-portion of an item's value in rela-tion to its weight. Because selling on eBay typically involves ship-ping the product to customers, which becomes more expensive the larger the item, it makes more financial sense to sell small items of high value than to sell large items of small value. A used pine desk is very heavy and would be very expensive to ship, but prob-ably wouldn't command a high price. Diamond earrings and rare stamps, on the other hand, have a very high value density.

listings only" box. You will see exactly which items sold, what they sold for, and how many bids there were.

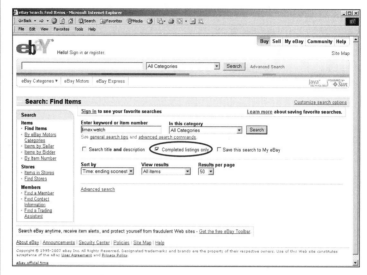

Enter keywords for an item and check the "Completed listings only" box to learn what similar merchandise has sold for.

Say you sell Timex Watches. Do an Advanced Search using the words "Timex watch" and indicate that you only want to see the completed listings. A screen will appear showing all the auctions that have closed in the last seven days that have those keywords in the title and/or description. Notice that you have access to everything from the listings (and photos) themselves to the number of bids to the final price. Shipping information will also be included, which can be very helpful when figuring out how much you can charge to ship similar items.

Do this kind of research for each type of item that you sell. And continually monitor it. Trends appear—and disappear. You must stay on top of your business at all times.

You can also pay to get access to completed listings for a longer range of time. And as you get serious about your eBay business, you will probably want to spend the money for this service. Information on completed listings for longer timeframes also gives you a better idea of whether there are seasonal variations in prices for your products as well as pricing trends over time.

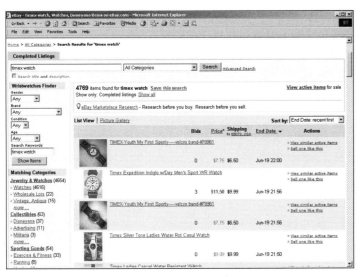

A Completed Listings result page for "Timex watch" shows what similar items sold for.

Track Completed Listing Prices

To get an idea of how much items like yours are selling for, fill out the following worksheet. Track prices of completed listings over the course of at least a few weeks. Take notes on the special features or conditions (if any) of each sale that might distinguish one item (or collection of items) from others in the same category. No matter what you *think* your merchandise is worth, this is the best way to learn what it could actually bring in.

DATE	ITEM	SELLING PRICE	SPECIAL FEATURES	NOTES

Calculate likely income

Once you've researched what items like yours have sold for recently, you can come up with a ballpark figure for the prices you are likely to get for your own auctions. Now comes the moment of truth: Are such prices high enough to cover all the expenses you estimated in Chapters 17 and 18? Even more importantly, will you move beyond break-even to the point of making a profit and earning an income for your time?

The following calculations will help you estimate your cash income and profit.

Gross Income

Your *gross income* is the total amount of money earned before *any* expenses are accounted for.

Estimated total number of items sold monthly:_____

Multiplied by

Estimated average sale price of each item before expenses:_____

Equals

Estimated monthly gross income: _____

Gross Profit

Your *gross profit* is the total amount of money earned after deducting expenses that are directly related to the sale—for instance, the cost of goods sold and your eBay expenses.

Estimated average sale price of each item on eBay:_____

Minus

Estimated average cost of purchasing or making each item:_____

Minus

Estimated average cost of eBay fees per item/sale:_____

Minus

Estimated average cost of other costs associated with sale of each item, if any:_____

Multiplied by

Number of items sold each month:_____

Equals

Estimated gross profit per month: _____

Net Profit

Your *net profit* is the total amount of money you have after subtracting all expenses (usually before taking income tax into account). This is the amount of money you will be able to pay yourself if it's a positive number—or the amount you'll need to borrow if it's a negative number.

Estimated *gross profit* per month: _____

Minus

Estimated monthly operating expenses: _____

Equals

Estimated monthly net profit: _____

If the net profit results are positive: Congratulations! You have a viable eBay business.

If the results are negative: You have several options:

■ **Look for alternate suppliers.** This may not be an option, especially if you create exquisite one-of-a-kind crafts or you sell collectibles that can only be found for less through rare strikes of luck. But sometimes being creative about *where* you get your items can make the difference between making it on eBay or not. Of course, if you choose this option, you'll have to be absolutely on top of all your expenses—if your margins start to slip, it might be time to try the last suggestion in this list.

■ **Reduce expenses.** If you can't increase income, you'll have to lower your expenses. This could mean eliminating some of the eBay selling features (if doing so doesn't cut into sales), cutting down on outside service providers, working from home, and the like.

■ **Come up with a new eBay idea.** Lots of sellers do this. Once they recognize the opportunities on eBay, they keep experimenting with different products until they find a niche that works.

Pricing Strategies

U ltimately, the market will set the price for your auction item. But the minimum price you set—and whether you decide to set a Reserve Price for your auction—can play a big role in how many bidders you get, and how high they go. Choose an eBay pricing strategy that best suits both the type of items you are selling and your own personal tolerance for risk. You have five choices:

■ **Set a low starting price for an auction.** This option is recommended by many eBay sellers (as well as eBay itself), because it encourages the largest number of buyers to bid on your product. A low starting price plays into the buyers' sense that they are snagging a great deal. Low starting prices often attract a flurry of bidders and bidding. Many people, once they are involved in an auction, like to stick with it until they "win." Be wary of this option if you are selling expensive one-of-a-kind items for which there may be few bidders, if you are selling

QUICK TIP

Starting and Reserve Price

The starting price is the price at which a seller wants bidding for an item to begin in an auction-style listing. The starting price may not necessarily be the lowest price the seller is willing to sell their item for. Sellers can also set a secret Reserve Price that represents the true minimum; if the high bid does not meet the Reserve Price, then the seller is under no obligation to sell the item to the bidder. This feature enables sellers to set a lower starting price to stimulate bidding among buyers.

a very expensive item where an extremely low starting price may make buyers wonder about the quality or authenticity of the item, or if you have had to spend a lot of money to acquire the item.

Let's say, for example, you are selling a new in box Tiffany-style table lamp that cost you $9 to acquire. Completed auctions indicate that this type of lamp generally sells for about $20 on eBay. By setting an initial starting price of $1.99, you are likely to attract many bidders.

- **Set a high(er) starting price for an auction.** This is the option to choose if you are nervous about covering your costs, even on relatively less expensive items. eBay sellers typically follow this strategy when they want to make sure they meet their basic expenses—that is, the cost of the item itself and all fees. Having a relatively high starting price may reduce the number of bidders and discourage frenzied bidding, but you're better protected from having to accept a final bid that is lower than your costs.

If it cost you $9 to acquire the Tiffany-style lamp and you will have to pay Insertion and Final Value Fees to eBay, you may decide to set an initial starting price of $12.99. This will reduce the number of bidders—and increase the possibility of lowering your final sale price—but you'll be assured of covering your expenses.

- **Use the Reserve pricing option.** Selling something rare or extremely valuable? The last thing you want to do is to have to sell it for far less than you could in the real world. To that end, some eBay sellers will set a Reserve Price (see page 139), the lowest price at which they will sell an item. If that price is not met, then the auction does not go through, thus guaranteeing the seller the appropriate profit on their item. The Reserve Price can be kept secret, but bidders will see that one has been set, or if you choose you can disclose the Reserve Price in your description.

Start Low, Sell Higher

There's some compelling evidence that your risks when starting an auction at a low price point are not as great as you might think. An August 2006 study by the Kellogg School of Management at Northwestern University, which examined buyer behavior during eBay auctions, found that auctions with lower starting prices actually ended up commanding higher amounts at the end of the bidding than those that started with higher price demands. The reason is a theory called "sunk costs": once someone invests the time and energy to take part in an auction, they become emotionally involved. They're psychologically committed precisely because they've put in this effort. That's why they keep bidding. Interestingly, the Kellogg research found that starting at a lower price works best for auctions in which there is a lot of interest. For those items that you expect will generate less demand, it's best to set a higher starting price.

The disadvantage of choosing this option, of course, is that it can discourage people from bidding. Many people do not like to bid on Reserve Price auctions and others are deterred by the uncertainty of not knowing the secret Reserve Price.

Once again, imagine an auction of a table lamp. But this time it is a genuine antique Tiffany lamp costing thousands of dollars. You are likely to want to set a Reserve Price for it so that you are assured of not letting go of a rare item for less than what it is worth.

■ **Select the Buy It Now option.** If you are fairly confident about the going market price of an item, and want to entice buyers who don't want to bother with the uncertainty of an actual auction, you can choose this strategy. With this option, you set the Buy It Now price at some point above (usually slightly above) your best guess of what the auction will pull in. This may encourage those teetering on the edge to make a commitment to purchase from you immediately rather than waiting for the auction to close. Buy It Now options are only available to eBay sellers after they have reached a certain feedback score, and there are additional fees for this option (see page 146).

If you have a number of brand new Tiffany-style lamps and know that they usually sell on eBay auctions for $19.99, you could offer them at an $18.99 Buy It Now price. Buyers would be interested because the price seems reasonable and they could avoid the hassle of an auction. But you'd probably make slightly less, and pay a bit more in eBay fees, than if you put them up for auction.

■ **Use Buy It Now in conjunction with Best Offer.** As an added incentive to get people to commit to buying your item without waiting for the auction to close, you can give them the chance to offer you what *they* feel the item is worth. Obviously, this offer will be above the current bid price (and the starting price you have set) but below your Buy It Now price. This is another strategy to get buyers to consider bidding on your wares (see page 147).

When you're new to eBay, you're probably going to want to try out a number of these pricing strategies to see which work best for you and your products. You'll learn which strategies bring you the best prices and which you're the most comfortable with.

Wisely choosing your pricing strategy—or strategies, as you may want to use a number of different ones depending on the items you're selling—contributes to your eBay success and profits. But it will take time to learn which strategies are best for you, so be patient.

When Should You Specify a Reserve?

When you opt for a reserve auction, you are basically setting a minimum price for your item, and reserving the right to withdraw the item if no one meets this price. You can keep this reserve secret—buyers can bid on your item, and will only be told "reserve not met" until someone hits the magic figure. You can always disclose the reserve amount, of course, if you feel that this will attract more buyers to the auction and discourage less serious bidders.

A reserve works best in cases where you want to minimize your risk. Say you are auctioning off a rare 17th century wooden flute that would retail for between $1,500 and $2,000 at an antique music store. The last thing you want is to have it go for $200! By setting the minimum amount you will accept, you are protecting yourself against catastrophes like that.

Be aware that some buyers are put off by reserve auctions because they feel that sellers who use them are trying to artificially inflate the prices of their items. This type of buyer prefers to know the minimum price you will accept before placing a bid.

Taking Care of Business

"*You should expect the same issues to arise on eBay as in a conventional store. It's just an ordinary course of business that some checks will bounce, some credit cards will be declined, and some items will be stolen. But that's just a very small percentage of the transactions on eBay. You can deal with these issues and still have a very profitable eBay business.*"

Stella Kleiman, BBB member,
eBay PowerSeller, and owner of FoundValue,
San Francisco, California

Making *the* Sale

Types of Auctions

Y our first sale will be an auction, since you can't offer Fixed Price sales until you've chalked up some experience with traditional eBay auctions. You'll have several options in an auction-type sale:

- Standard auction
- Reserve Price auction
- Multiple Item (Dutch) auction
- Restricted Access auction
- Private auction

Standard (traditional) auctions

This is the most basic and common way to sell on eBay. You list your item, allow bids to come in for a specified amount of time, then award the item to the highest bidder. This is the type of transaction that most people think of when they think of eBay—and it is how eBay first began. Everything else came later. This style of transaction is best understood by both buyers and sellers. It is very straightforward, and not intimidating, as it mirrors the way auctions are conducted in the real, physical world.

QUICK TIP

Start Small

To quickly get to the point where you can offer Fixed Price and Buy It Now items, start out by auctioning a number of less expensive items—anything will do—to get your positive feedback numbers up. Do a great job, give superb customer service, and in no time at all you'll be qualified to offer advanced eBay features.

Reserve Price auctions

Although in any auction you specify a minimum price—you can go as low as 99 cents—sometimes you may also want to set a Reserve Price. This is the minimum price you are willing to accept for an item, and, most importantly, it is a secret. Bidders on the item won't know what the reserve is (unless you tell them) until it is met; instead, they will merely get a "reserve not met" message when they submit a bid.

You might wonder why there would be the need for a reserve auction when you can already specify a minimum bid. Why not simply set a starting price that represents the lowest bid you will accept? Usually, that strategy works fine—unless the lowest bid you will accept is a very high figure. In such cases, a large initial price can scare away prospective bidders, many of whom are searching for bargains. They will be hesitant to even try bidding on an item that will obviously be sold at regular market rates.

Yet if you sell valuable items—say, rare vintage vinyl records—you won't want to accept less for them than you could get on the retail market. Otherwise, what's the point of using eBay as a market? A Reserve Price auction can seem like a very safe way to put rare or expensive items on the market.

But there's a drawback: the fact that the reserve is kept secret can scare off potential bidders, who feel unsure of the terrain they are treading on. You can alleviate that uncertainty by specifying the reserve in your item description, but then you are back to the issue of seeming to ask too much upfront. To reassure nervous bidders, you may want to talk about the price they might pay in a store for the same item as the one in your description.

Reserve Price auctions work best when you are offering very rare items, like antiques, art, or valuable collectables, or very expensive items such as cars, boats, industrial

Shills

Something that is forbidden on eBay (and indeed, in any auction, online or traditional) is *shilling*—attempting to start a bidding war by submitting phony bids. In online auctions, sellers do this by creating multiple accounts and using them to place bids, making it appear as if a number of different people are eager to acquire the product. They may also recruit friends or relatives with no intention of purchasing an item to bid on it to drive up the price.

Besides being illegal (you can go to jail for fraud), there are financial risks attached to shilling; there is always the chance that sellers who engage in this activity, rather than driving the price up, get stuck with their own merchandise. Because they still have to pay all the eBay fees—which can be considerable, based on the "winning" bid the seller submitted—this type of activity can be a costly, as well as unethical, gamble. Shilling is against eBay rules, and can result in your account being suspended indefinitely or revoked altogether.

equipment, jewelry, and high-end electronics. Reserve Price auctions are also a good idea when you are first testing the eBay market for rare or expensive goods, or you have items you don't want to part with unless you get a certain price.

Multiple Item auctions

Say you have more than one of an item. This is a very common situation if you build your eBay business around purchasing items in lots. Unless you want to take on the time-consuming job of listing each of the digital clock radios you acquired separately, you can offer buyers a Multiple Item (or Dutch) auction. Unlike traditional auctions, Dutch auctions can have multiple winners.

You list the items just as you would in a traditional auction, only you check off the Multiple Item box and say what quantity you are trying to sell. The listing fee, just as with a traditional auction, is based upon the minimum bid price you set, but is multiplied by the number of items you are selling.

Dutch auctions are very different from single-item auctions in that the bidder must specify how many items they want to buy in addition to how much they are willing to pay for each one. And although highest bidders win the *quantity* they want, when the auction closes all the winning bidders pay the same *price* per item—and that price is the *lowest* winning bid.

Confused? Say that you are selling 10 digital clock radios. Bidding is steady; you have three bidders who seem especially interested, as they keep topping each others' bids. At the close of the auction, the winning bid is defined by the highest bid price *per item,* not the highest total amount. For example, a bid to buy three of your clock radios at $21 per item (for a total of $63) will win over a bid to purchase five of them at $20 each (for a total of $100). Thus the winner gets to purchase three of your radios.

But wait—here's the somewhat confusing part. The winning bidder offered $21 each for three radios; the second-highest bidder offered $20 each for five radios. That leaves two radios—and so the third-highest bidder gets those. But that bidder only offered $10 per radio. In such cases, all three winners get the items at the lowest bid at which you still have radios to sell—and that's just $10 each. So you will end up selling all 10 radios at $10 each.

You can see the advantages and disadvantages of this method of selling right away. You have the convenience of auctioning off a lot of items in one easy transaction, but you risk getting less per item than some buyers are willing to pay.

Restricted Access auctions

eBay includes a category called Mature Audiences that sells items considered to be of an adult nature. Although eBay specifically states that it doesn't take a moral stand on the sale (or purchase) of such items, it *does* separate them from the rest of the site. Only users who have had their age verified through the "ID Verify" feature (see page 190) can access this category.

A Restricted Access auction makes it easy for your buyers to find—or avoid—adult-only items. Sellers and buyers need to put a credit card on file with eBay before being allowed to list or bid on a Mature Audience item as a Restricted Access auction. Moreover, items listed on Restricted Access auctions are not accessible through keyword searches.

Private Listing auctions

Sometimes you'll want to list an item in a private auction, which means that bidders' names (eBay IDs) won't be displayed, either during the bidding or when the auction closes. As the seller, you are the only person who will know the would-be buyers' IDs.

You would choose to hold a private auction if the item in question is very unusual or rare, or if you think it will go for a very high price. In this way, eBay is very much like the top traditional auction houses, where the bidding is done by proxy and is frequently anonymous. For example, a famous work of art will be sold, but no one will be sure exactly who bought it. It's the same on eBay. If you deal with objects that are of extreme interest to a limited number of collectors, they may want their identities kept secret. Holding a private auction is the best way to appeal to this type of buyer. (However, since the bidders' identities aren't shown, some potential bidders may be fearful of shills.)

Auction Types

AUCTION TYPE	PROS	CONS
Standard auction	eBay community is familiar with it; standard and easy way to proceed with routine items.	Doesn't always meet your needs if you have rare or expensive items or a special community of buyers.
Reserve Price auction	Guarantees that you won't have to part with a valuable item for less than you're willing to accept.	The uncertainty can scare off and frustrate potential buyers.
Multiple Item auction	You don't have to create separate listings for a lot of identical items.	You may get lower total revenues than you would get by selling items separately.
Restricted Access auction	People specifically looking for "adult only" items can find you quickly.	None if you sell this type of item. It's the only way you can sell certain goods on eBay.
Private Listing auction	Buyers who want to protect their privacy can bid with confidence.	None if you sell items for which bidders want to remain anonymous. May scare off traditional eBay bidders.

Limiting Bidders on Your Listings

You don't have to do business with everyone in the eBay community. eBay provides sellers with a number of tools to help them feel comfortable with their transaction partners. It offers ways to include or exclude certain members from participating in your particular auctions or Buy It Now sales. These include:

■ **Adding eBay members to your "blocked" list.** If you know that you don't want to sell to certain eBay members, and you know their eBay member IDs, you can put them on your blocked list. Anyone you put on that list cannot bid on *any* of your listings, and, if you are especially picky about who you do business with, you can block as many as 1,000 eBay members from your auctions. This is a way of blocking competitors or buyers you've had problems with in the past. (However, be careful that you don't block so many members that you drastically limit the number of potential buyers. This is especially true if you're selling specialized goods to a limited market.)

■ **Pre-approving bidders and buyers.** You can also create a pre-approved bidder/buyer list for any item and only allow those on your list to bid. If someone who is *not* on your pre-approved list wants to bid on your item, they can send you an email so that you can consider their request. You are allowed to add or delete approved bidders up to the second your pre-approved listing ends. This technique may reduce the number of potential bidders for your item, as some will not bother to contact you.

■ **Canceling bids.** Although not encouraged by eBay, it is possible to cancel bids. According to eBay, there are three "legitimate" reasons to do this:

1) A bidder directly sends you an email asking to be released from a bid. You don't have to do it, according to eBay rules, but depending on the circumstances—and how much a bidder pleads for clemency—you may choose to accept the request.

2) You are worried about the legitimacy of a bidder and try to verify their identity. But after attempting all reasonable means of trying to reach them without success, you decide to cancel their bid rather than face the possibility of dealing with a deadbeat or scammer.

3) You check on the feedback rating of your bidders and discover that one of them has a very negative rating for failing to pay for items won in the past. You prefer to cancel the bid rather than face the potential hassle and cost of dealing with a deadbeat.

■ **Buyer requirements.** Even if you don't have specific users you'd like to eliminate from bidding on your items, you might want to provide a *general* profile outlining who can and can't participate in your auctions. You do this by specifying "buyer requirements."

Buyer requirements allow you to block buyers from bidding on or purchasing your items based on a number of characteristics, including whether a buyer:

● Is registered in a country to which you don't ship

● Has a negative feedback score

● Has received any Unpaid Item "strikes"

● Does not have a PayPal account

Fixed Price Sales

In addition to the regular auctions that are at the heart of the eBay system, you have the option of selling things at fixed prices. With a Fixed Price format, you can sell your items immediately at a price you set yourself—there's no need to wait for an auction to end. Using this sales format for your eBay business will attract a different kind of buyer: one who doesn't like the uncertainty of a regular auction and is perhaps willing to pay a little more to eliminate that uncertainty.

Buy It Now and other Fixed Price sales have slightly higher fees than standard auctions. Based upon the final selling price of the item, these fees range from pennies up to several dollars.

Even though they are not auctions, Fixed Price listings with a Buy It Now price still show up when buyers browse regular categories as well as on the Search Results page. A special icon shows up next to the title of your item. Additionally, your items will be listed on the Buy It Now tab on the Search Results page.

A Fixed Price sale screen.

Fixed Price sales, like reserve auctions, are well suited to sellers who want to minimize the risk of having items go for much less than they are worth on the market. They're also good for those who have items likely to appeal to those who don't want to participate in auctions (such as ticket buyers) or to sellers who don't want to deal with the auction format. Items listed in the Fixed Price format have the same Insertion and Final Value fees as online auction listings. The fee amount is based on the Buy It Now price you set.

QUICK TIP

The PayPal Advantage

If you want to offer a single item at a fixed price, you must have at least 10 buyers who have given you feedback, or be ID Verified (see page 190). However, if you have a PayPal account, you can offer a Fixed Price sale with a feedback rating of just five.

Buy It Now

There are three ways you can offer your buyers an item at a fixed price: Buy It Now (auction format), Buy It Now (Fixed Price format only), and Buy It Now (eBay Stores).

- **Auction format.** In this form of Buy It Now, you offer the option alongside a regular auction. Buyers will have the choice of buying your item immediately or placing a bid on your item. However, this option is only available before a bid has been placed or before a reserve price has been met. Once actual bidding begins, or the bidding surpasses the Reserve Price, the Buy It Now option is no longer available. There is an additional fee for auction listings that include the Buy It Now feature.

- **Fixed Price format only.** With this variation of Buy It Now, you are making would-be buyers a straight offer: get this item for a specified price. There is no option of also bidding on the item—what buyers see is what they get.

- **eBay Store item format.** If you have an eBay Store (see page 186), you can also list a store item at a fixed price. The listing will *only* appear in your eBay Store, not on the Category or Search Results pages. As with Fixed Price format Buy It Now listings, buyers have the opportunity to buy your item(s) at the prices you have set, but there is no option for bidding. If you have more than one identical item, you can sell them both within a single listing.

QUICK TIP

Shipping with Best Offer

If you previously stated the shipping costs for an item in your Best Offer listing, that fee is not negotiable. But if you have not specified any shipping fees, the buyer can ask to have shipping included in their Best Offer price. They will check the "Including shipping" box in the offer message. Pay attention to that when deciding whether to accept or reject their offer.

Best Offer

Sometimes you might *really* want to make a sale. Perhaps you have a large supply of overstock inventory, or last year's merchandise, or perishable items (including tickets for soon-to-be-held events). In cases like these you might be willing to immediately accept any good offer. The Best Offer feature can be used with any Fixed Price format listing (not with auctions, however). No matter what price you have listed, buyers can contact you to tell you what they would be willing to pay for your item. Best Offer would also be a good choice for you if you had already chosen to offer a Fixed Price auction to avoid the risk of too-low bids, but if you are actually willing to accept less.

Individual buyers can only make one Best Offer for your item. Just as with regular auction bids, each offer is binding on the buyer. Best offers are valid for 48 hours. As a seller, you have four options for responding if a buyer decides to make you an offer:

- **Accept it.** The person who made the offer is the immediate winner of the item. You notify them that they have won, and you complete the deal just like any other eBay transaction. If there are any other buyers who have submitted bids, their offers will automatically be declined.

- **Decline it.** This is always your right, but for courtesy's sake, be sure to tell the buyer why the offer was not accepted. Be polite, even if the offer is ridiculously low.

- **Let the offer expire.** It will do so after 48 hours. However, to be a good member of the eBay community, it is always considerate to respond in some way to an offer.

- **Make a counteroffer.** If you receive a Best Offer that is close to what you can accept, you may want to go back to the buyer and say that, for slightly more money, the item can be theirs.

Require Immediate Payment

If you decide to go the Buy It Now route, you can require that the buyer use PayPal to pay you immediately. This is an especially valuable feature if you sell items that have a time limit on them, such as tickets to sporting events or concerts.

Using this feature, once buyers have clicked on the Pay It Now button, they are sent to the payment page, where they must pay immediately using PayPal. Until they pay, the item is still technically available to others—such as people who wish to bid on it in an auction (depending on which Buy It Now format you chose) or someone else who clicks on the Buy It Now button. According to eBay rules, the Buy It Now transaction is not over until the buyer has paid using PayPal.

You can take advantage of the immediate payment requirement with any item that has a Buy It Now price attached to it. But there are restrictions: you have to have a PayPal Premier or PayPal Business account when you list your item. Also, the Buy It Now price must be less than $4,000, and you need to make the shipping charges—plus any other costs—clear in your listing.

Auction Timing

T iming matters—a lot. If you watch other auctions, you'll notice that the bidding can be very slow at first—but then, in the last few minutes of the auction, bidding can break out and go crazy. That's often because of snipers (see page 151), who wait until the last possible moment to place their bids, as well as because the people who have been bidding all along are responding to the late arrivals to the party.

Daily and hourly variations

The day, or even the hour, that your auction ends can make a huge difference to your returns. Indeed, the top eBay sellers devote significant amounts of time to analyzing the best time to list, as it can make a difference between mediocre and satisfying financial results.

■ **List at a time that is reasonable for bidders in most U.S. time zones.** The time you place your listing matters because it determines when your listing will end: either 3, 5, 7, or 10 days from the moment you push the button. Keep in mind that not every would-be buyer is going to be in your time zone! (eBay is international in scope, but trying to accommodate all global time zones would be difficult, if not impossible.)

Having an auction end at 10 a.m. Eastern time might seem reasonable to you—but at that moment it would only be 7 a.m. on the west coast, and some very interested bidders might not even have had their morning cup of coffee yet.

You may think that ending an auction at 9 p.m. Pacific time makes sense—but that's midnight on the east coast, which might prevent some people from participating when the bidding gets hot and heavy at the last moment.

■ **End at a time appropriate to the demographics of your target audience.** If you're trying to appeal to an elderly demographic, you probably won't want your listing to end very late in the evening. If you're going for a younger audience, you might be well served assuming that Friday and Saturday nights are not the best time to begin or end listings.

If you're selling industrial or business supplies, however, timing your auction to end during working hours on a weekday may prove most fruitful.

■ **Choose the best day to end your auction.** Most auction activity on eBay takes place over weekends; thus, Sunday, when many potential buyers are home by their computers, is the best day to end an auction. End your auction at a time that works for buyers across the continental United States—7 or 8 p.m. (Eastern time) on a Sunday is usually a good bet.

■ **Pay attention to holidays as well as special events,** like big football games or Hollywood awards nights, and avoid ending auctions while these are underway. Your buyers are more likely to be away from their computers.

Not all of these generalizations will apply to you and your auctions. Do your own research and find out when the most bidding and buying activity for items like yours takes place. And make sure your auctions won't end while you're on vacation or away from your computer for many days. You will be unavailable to answer questions and might also be late in sending the merchandise to the winning bidder. This could result in negative feedback for you.

Experiment with Auction Length

Experiment with auction duration—trying all possible options and combinations—to see whether it makes any difference at all to your profitability.

Seasonal variations

Just like at brick-and-mortar retail stores, some times are better than others to sell particular items on eBay. Take the holiday season (between Thanksgiving and Christmas). That's the busiest time of year for all stores—online and offline—and you should expect to devote considerably more time and energy to your eBay business at this critical time than during other months. You might also consider subscribing to eBay's Gift Services feature during this time (see page 101). It will cost you extra but can be well worth the investment by increasing the number of people you attract to your listings.

January and February are traditionally slower times for most retail businesses. That's when brick-and-mortar stores hold sales, do promotions, and use all the marketing tools at their disposal to attract buyers into their stores. You can do the same.

If you only offer traditional auctions, you should expect less bidding and lower final prices during these months. This is a time when many sellers increase their starting prices in order to avoid having to part with items for too little. You may even want to withhold certain items from auction during these slow months, especially if you're worried that you won't cover your costs.

If you use Buy It Now or other Fixed Price selling strategies, you can lower your prices early in the year in order to attract buyers. You should also expect to get lower Best Offers—and whether or not you accept them depends on your business model.

Of course, none of this may apply if you sell items that have seasonal appeal. Ski and snowboarding equipment will do better in winter. Hiking, swimming, boating, and other warm-weather gear will do better in spring and summer. However, as a *buyer*—that is, as you source items that you will later put on eBay for sale—you will want to use "off" months to increase your inventory.

Auction duration

You have four options to choose from when determining the duration of your auction: 3, 5, 7, and 10 days. Many eBay buyers don't log on every day, so it makes sense to have your listing available for all seven days of the week. Three-day auctions will speed up your sales cycle and bring in money sooner, but you may forfeit some profit because your auctions will have less exposure. However, if a holiday is approaching and you have an item that you know will be in high demand—say, Valentine's Day jewelry—a short auction time may be just what last-minute buyers are looking for.

Ten-day auctions—which eBay will charge more for—are best suited to very expensive, rare items like antiques, art, and valuable collectibles, as they give collectors and other specialty buyers adequate time to learn about the auction and prepare their bidding strategies.

Give Your Buyers a Full Week

For most items, seven-day listings tend to work best, as they provide buyers with adequate time to consider your item, but don't make them impatient that the process is dragging out too long.

Sniping

Sniping is a popular strategy used by buyers trying to win auctions—and it's not necessarily a good thing for sellers.

When a buyer watches an auction closely but doesn't bid until the very last moment before the auction closes, that's sniping. Some buyers do this by sitting at their keyboards and trying to time their bids to the final minutes. Others use online sniping services that automatically place bids in the last *seconds* of an auction. (These services charge buyers only if they win an auction.)

Many buyers resent sniping, as it gives them no chance to respond to last-minute bids with higher offers of their own. But it is sellers who have the most objections. In a traditional face-to-face auction, the gavel isn't struck until the last bid has trickled in—no matter how long it takes. But in eBay's timed auction, there is an established, non-negotiable end to the bidding. Sniping thus puts an artificial "cap" on what you, the seller, might get for an item, especially during very heated and competitive auctions.

Although some online auctions forbid sniping and have put processes in place to make it impossible, eBay does not have a policy against it. The only thing you can do to protect yourself against sniping is to set a reserve price. That way, you will at least be assured of receiving the minimum price you will accept.

Communicate, Communicate, Communicate

E ven before your auction ends, you need to start delivering stellar customer service. This might sound contradictory. After all, bidders aren't technically your customers—yet. But the customer experience begins the very first time a would-be buyer clicks on the title of your listing to investigate further. If it's poorly written or unprofessional sounding, they may not proceed further. If attracted by your listing, however, they may have questions about your item that they need answered before they will consider bidding on it. And this is where the real work of proving yourself a responsive seller comes into play.

Respond quickly

One of the biggest fallacies about running an eBay business is that the auctions will take care of themselves. Nothing could be further from the truth. Bidders want—and, indeed, expect—prompt responses to their pre-bidding questions. If you wait 24 hours before you send a reply, you may well

QUICK TIP

Get Email on Your Cell Phone

Email is a standard feature on many cell phones and PDAs. Once you start your eBay business, if things go well and volume picks up, you may want to stay in closer touch with your customer base than you can using only your computer. Having a service that allows you to pick up email messages from your cell phone or PDA may become a business necessity.

have lost a bidder. They may move on to an auction where a similar item is being offered by a more responsive seller. Or they might just steer away from any auction in which the seller doesn't demonstrate a commitment to the merchandise, worrying that it reflects on the way that seller will ship and provide follow-up support for the item.

When responding to a buyer's inquiry, always:

- **Answer the question.** Don't beat around the bush or wander off subject. Directly address the specific question the buyer has asked. Be thorough in your answer, but there's no need to provide a Ph.D. thesis — the buyer can ask more questions if your answer is not satisfactory. Don't hide anything or deliberately omit important information. If you don't know the answer to a question, or a part of a question — say you don't know for sure how old that antique-looking Mexican religious painting is — say so. Buyers appreciate, and reward, honesty.

- **Add the question (and your answer) to the Ask the Seller a Question page.** Chances are good that if one buyer has a question, others will have similar ones. Save yourself some time by publicly posting the question and related answer on your Ask the Seller a Question page. Seeing that you have been open and honest with others can cause buyers to have more confidence in your item — and in you.

- **Engage in a dialogue if the buyer wishes it.** Don't get impatient if a buyer comes back with an additional question or asks you to clarify something you've already said. Unless it becomes clear after an extended exchange that the buyer isn't paying attention to your answers, always be polite and responsive to follow-up issues that the buyer raises. The most serious and interested buyers — especially for higher-priced items — are likely to have the most questions.

Answering Buyers' Emails

You'll only be able to answer a question from a buyer once. If you have already answered a question and want to provide additional information, or modify what you said, you must use eBay's *email forwarding system* (see page 155). Above all, be responsive! You can easily lose buyers by failing to respond promptly and courteously to requests for information.

Creating Frequently Asked Questions (FAQs)

You may find, after you've sold a few items, that a number of questions are asked time and time again. You can create a list of FAQs that interested buyers will see when they go to the Ask Seller a Question link. Having an FAQ list not only saves you time but is likely to increase the number of bidders you get, as the fact that you have already anticipated and answered their questions will increase potential bidders' confidence in you.

Some of the information that you might want to include in your FAQs list:

- Your return policy

- Explanation of your processing and handling fees

- Requirements that buyers purchase insurance

- Special shipping considerations

- Answers to questions specific to the merchandise you are selling that arise frequently

- General information about your business, or personal background, that you feel will be of interest to buyers

Displaying questions and answers

Additionally, you may be asked a question about an item that you think other buyers may be interested in. You can post the question and your answer on your View Item page as well as on the Ask Seller a Question page. You can show up to 100 questions and answers on your item page.

NOTE: Once the question is posted online, it cannot be removed or edited. So post carefully!

Hiding your email address

eBay is very conscious of protecting the identity of both buyers and sellers. By using the eBay email forwarding system to communicate, neither party in a transaction reveals their personal email address—the only thing each correspondent knows is the other person's eBay user name. Messages are sent through the eBay email system, and eBay forwards the message to the other person. However, at any time, either party can choose to reveal their own email address so as to facilitate more direct communication.

Although buyers won't be able to see your email address on your listing, when you respond to any questions they have they *will* see your email, just as they would if you sent an email from your account under regular circumstances. You can hide your email address when responding to eBay queries merely by checking the box that says "Hide my email address from <buyer username>." Your response will then be sent to the interested buyer without your email address on it, and the buyer will need to use the Ask Seller a Question link on your item page if they want to communicate with you again.

INSIDER'S INSIGHT

Fraudulent Emails

Never open any emails that are supposedly about a recent transaction that look as though they come from eBay or PayPal, but which are sent to your regular email address. Always use the PayPal and eBay websites to pick up your messages. Otherwise, you'll be taken to a fake website where scammers will try and get your personal information, and you could lose a lot of money.

Jim Nieciecki, BBB member, eBay PowerSeller, and Owner of Federation Toys, Hoffman Estates, Illinois

Playing It Safe

"Your biggest risk on eBay is how to accept payment. You should never, ever ship something before payment has cleared. Actually, we stopped accepting personal checks some time ago. If they don't do PayPal, we ask them for a money order so we're actually paid in cash."

Chad Bryant, BBB member,
eBay PowerSeller, and owner of Red Raven Press,
Windsor, Colorado

After *the* Auction

Payment

T he final virtual gavel has been struck, and your auction is finally over. It's time to collect your money and ship your item to the winning bidder. Here's how the process works.

eBay sends you an end-of-auction email

Moments after your auction ends, you will receive an end-of-auction email from eBay that informs you about all the details of the transaction: the winning bid, the winning bidder, and a summary of all the activity on the auction.

The buyer gets a similar email that also includes a summary of the eBay rules for paying for the items they have won.

Send the winning bidder an email

The first thing to do is communicate with your buyers. Send a courteous congratulatory message stating that they have won the auction and specifying your policies for getting paid, as well as details about when and how you will ship the product to them. This message should include:

■ Acknowledgement of the final price of the auction

■ Reminder of when payment is due (can be any time up to 45 days)

■ Shipping fees (if applicable)

■ Policy on insurance for shipping (if applicable)

■ Return policy

■ Total cost of item to be paid

■ Choice of payment options: personal check, money order/cashier's check, credit card, or PayPal

Receive payment

Some buyers are very meticulous and—if you offer PayPal as an option—push the PayPal payment button immediately so that you receive your money within minutes of the auction closing. If your buyer chooses to pay by personal check or money order, you will have to wait—sometimes quite a long time—to get paid. After all, it can take time before the buyer actually sits down to write the check—or goes to the bank to buy the money order/cashier's check—and posts it to you. Then you have to wait until the check clears.

Of course, many buyers are motivated to pay you so they can get the item right away. But there *are* laggards as well as deadbeats who don't pay at all. So the time between the end of the auction end and when you receive payment can be the most suspenseful part of the entire eBay experience.

Wait for payment to clear

If you accept checks as payment, it's essential that you do *not* ship your item until payment has cleared. Indeed, many sellers would prefer not to accept personal checks as payment because of the risks involved, but that would limit the number of potential bidders, as some buyers will *only* pay by check.

Waiting for a check to clear involves waiting an additional 7 to 10 days until your bank can verify that the funds have been successfully transferred to your account. You should, however, make this policy very clear in your listing or FAQs, as you don't want buyers to be disappointed because they wanted or needed the merchandise much sooner. After you've been running your eBay business for a while, however, you're likely to have many financial transactions with the same customers. As you come to trust them more, you may become slightly more flexible in your payment arrangements.

Avoid Overpayment Scams

One of the main scams going around involves someone who is interested or pretends to be interested in a car, and sends a fake cashier's check that overpays on the amount—say $15,000 instead of $10,000—and asks for $5,000 back. If you fall for that, you end up with a bogus check and are out $5,000 in addition to the vehicle. Even though cashier's checks and money orders are supposed to be safe, we always wait until they have cleared before we'll release a car or send a title.

Chris Lawler,
BBB member, eBay PowerSeller,
and owner of Redlaw Motors,
Fort Wayne, Indiana

Dealing with Deadbeats

Unfortunately, deadbeats—or people who win auctions and then refuse to pay, or just seem to disappear from the face of the earth—are out there, and if your eBay business thrives, you are almost certain to encounter one. When bidding on an item, buyers agree to a legally binding contract with eBay to purchase the item if they win the auction. If a winning bidder fails or refuses to pay, sellers can file an Unpaid Item dispute; eBay will then put a "strike" against the buyer's account. If there are too many strikes against a particular buyer within a particular time period—the exact number of strikes and time period are at eBay's discretion—a buyer's account will be suspended indefinitely.

Sellers can file an Unpaid Item dispute as soon as 7 days and up to 45 days after the auction closes. If they decide to relist the item for sale, they qualify for an Insertion Fee credit that basically means they can relist the item for free.

Bounced Checks

Many eBay sellers have encountered instances when a check for an item does not clear. If this happens to you, your first step will be to contact the buyer and inform them—courteously—about what has happened. After all, even the most honest people occasionally bounce checks, and you owe it to your buyer to provide the opportunity to set things right.

If the buyer does not respond to your initial email, you should send a second notice that repeats what the first notice says, adding that if you don't get a response within a certain period, you will void the auction.

Your third notice will inform the buyer that the auction has been cancelled. eBay has a process you can follow to report that an auction was not successfully completed (see sidebar) and to request a credit for the Final Value Fee you were charged. You then have the option of selling the item to the second highest bidder or relisting your item. You also have to decide at this point whether you will leave negative feedback for this particular eBay member. There are pros and cons to doing so, as outlined on page 183.

Packing and Shipping

A transaction is not complete until the buyer has received the item they won in an auction. And one of the biggest logistical and financial challenges for profitably operating an eBay business involves packing and shipping items that you have sold.

First, there's the actual cost of the packing materials. Then there are the shipping fees. Then there's the time it takes to prepare the product for shipping—which can be quite lengthy depending on the size, shape, or fragility of the item in question. Then you have to actually get the item into the hands of the U.S. Postal Service (USPS), UPS, FedEx, or other shipping firm. Finally, you have to follow up to make sure the buyer actually received the item in question.

If this sounds like a lot of work, that's because it is: in fact, one of the main obstacles that people face when taking their eBay businesses to the next level is figuring out efficient and cost-effective ways to streamline the packing and shipping process.

Upgrade Shipping, Increase Customer Satisfaction

People really like to get free or cheap shipping. I automatically upgrade all my customers to priority shipping for free. The cost differential is so small—just $1 for my training DVDs—and the customers love it. It boils down to two words: customer service.

Zain Naboulsi, BBB member, eBay PowerSeller, and owner of Insert Knowledge Here, Mansfield, Texas

Offer Priority Shipping

Buyers often appreciate having shipping options. You should therefore be very clear about *how* you will ship to them. Some sellers will only ship through the standard USPS service. Others will send items Priority Mail. Still others will offer UPS or FedEx shipping for an additional fee. This is often appreciated—especially during the holiday season, when people are anxious to get their hands on items they intend to use as gifts.

Shipping costs

One of the most important things you need to specify in your listing is how much it will cost the buyer to actually receive the item over and above the amount of the winning bid. There are two ways to do this: by specifying a flat shipping cost or by using eBay's Shipping Calculator to let buyers know exactly what they will pay, given their geographic location and other shipping preferences.

■ **Flat shipping costs**. You can decide to charge the buyer a flat fee to ship the item, regardless of the destination. You do this when you create your listing by entering the amount you will charge when prompted during the listing process. The fee you enter will display on your listing.

When deciding what to charge, you will probably first want to do some research into what it will actually cost to ship. You can use eBay's free Shipping Calculator (*http://payments.ebay.com/ws/ eBayISAPI.dll?EmitSellerShippingCalculator*) to get fairly accurate costs for both domestic and international destinations, and use this as the basis for what you will charge for shipping. Many sellers then add a "handling" fee on top of this to cover the time it takes them to prepare the item for shipment and arrange for it to be picked up by the shipping firm. This is perfectly acceptable as long as you respect eBay's prohibition against excessive shipping costs (see page 163).

QUICK TIP

The eBay Shipping Center

Precisely because shipping is such a big deal, eBay has gone to enormous lengths to provide tools to make it as painless as possible. Going to the eBay Shipping Center (*http://pages.ebay. com/services/buyandsell/shipping.html*) will give you access to a wealth of information and tools that should help you meet your shipping obligations efficiently and cost-effectively as your business grows.

■ **Calculated shipping costs.** Alternatively, you can allow eBay to automatically calculate U.S. Postal Service and UPS shipping costs for your buyers. Because shipping costs can vary by the buyer's location, this can more precisely cover all your shipping costs. You do this by choosing the "Calculated: Cost varies by buyer location" option in the Shipping section of the Sell Your Item form. You'll need to be very precise about the item weight and package size. You'll also need to specify which shipping service you will use (USPS or UPS) and your zip code. You also have the option, as with a flat fee, of adding in a handling cost.

If you choose this option, once an auction closes (or the buyer agrees to a Buy It Now transaction) and the buyer enters their zip code, a table of shipping rates will display. Any packaging or handling fees will automatically be included without disclosing to the buyer what those are—in other words, they simply see the total cost without any breakdown between shipping and handling. If you or the buyer decide to include insurance, this is added last—based on the final overall cost of the item plus shipping and handling—and displayed as a separate line item.

eBay's Excessive Shipping Policy

It is perfectly acceptable for you to charge an extra fee to cover all the costs of shipping—which include packaging as well as your (or your employees') time to pack the item so that it arrives safely. eBay does not have any firm limits on what constitutes an "acceptable" handling fee, but will actively investigate buyer complaints that shipping/handling charges are "excessive." The only hard and fast rules are that such fees cannot be calculated as a percentage of the final sale price, and that sellers offering insurance can only use licensed third-party insurance companies and can only charge the actual insurance cost. No "self insurance" or markup of insurance costs is permitted.

To be safe, you might want to be very conservative about what you charge, sticking to the actual out-of-pocket costs of shipping services plus packaging materials. Failure to comply with eBay's guidelines can result in anything from the cancellation of the listing to suspension of your account.

QUICK TIP

Offer Free Shipping

One sure way to attract more buyers is to offer free shipping. To help you spread the word that are you offering this perk, eBay has a Free Shipping filter that allows buyers to search only for listings that will ship items for free. This is an especially powerful selling tool during the holidays, when many non-eBay online merchants offer similar services.

eBay Shipping Tools

To expedite shipping, you can take advantage of the host of eBay Shipping Tools that you can access right from your desktop:

- **Print shipping and postage labels right from your computer.** You can purchase your shipping labels online and print them on your own printer—no special equipment or trips to the post office or UPS Store are required. This saves you the time of hand-addressing packages, typing shipping information into third-party label-generation software, and periodically having to do a postage run or go to a shipping office and deal with lines and clerks.

- **Insure your packages with a click of a mouse.** If using the USPS, you can purchase up to $500 in shipping insurance while preparing your labels. If you are shipping via UPS, each UPS domestic package or international shipment is automatically protected by UPS against loss or damage up to a value of $100. For items over $100, shippers may declare a value up to $999 when printing labels through PayPal.

- **Pay with PayPal.** You can pay for postage and shipping fees using your PayPal account. If you have a UPS account, you have the option of billing to it when you prepare your labels.

- **Print international labels and customs forms.** You can print international shipping labels from PayPal to serve your global buyers. Not only is the buyer's international address already filled in on the shipping label, but you can easily complete and print the required customs forms online.

- **Request a pickup from USPS or UPS.** After you have printed your label, simply request a pickup from USPS or UPS in order to save gas and a trip to the post office or UPS location. (NOTE: USPS free carrier pickup can only be used if you are shipping at least one Priority Mail or Express Mail package.) You and your buyer can then track the package through My eBay or PayPal.

- **Fewer buyer emails.** An email is automatically sent to both you and the buyer when you purchase a shipping label through eBay and PayPal. The email includes details on how the buyer can track the package. You'll therefore get fewer questions from buyers about the status of their shipments.

- **Competitive rates.** Both the USPS and UPS offer benefits when you purchase and print shipping labels online. USPS offers free delivery confirmation for Priority Mail and Express Mail packages, and lower-cost delivery confirmation for First Class, Media Mail, and Parcel Post packages. UPS offers lower shipping rates online than at the drop-off counter.

Shipping discounts

Shipping discounts let you offer buyers savings on shipping when they purchase multiple items from you. This can help you sell more items to the same buyer. You set your shipping discounts in My eBay under Preferences, and you can specify anything you want. For example, you can say that any purchases over $100 will result in free shipping—or will ship for a flat fee of $10.

Listings with shipping discounts appear to buyers with the message, "Save on shipping." When buyers pay for more than one item and your shipping discounts are set up and activated, eBay will automatically calculate the shipping discount, deduct it from the full shipping cost, and show the discount to buyers after they have paid for an item.

QUICK TIP

Free Co-Branded Shipping Suppliers

Make sure you take advantage of the free co-branded shipping boxes from the USPS for Priority Mail and Priority Mail Flat Rate Service boxes. These boxes come preprinted with the eBay logo and are delivered directly to your home free. To order boxes, go to *http://ebaysupplies.usps.com*.

International shipping

International shipping costs are based on a combination of the following:

- Weight and dimensions of the package
- Method of shipment (such as ground, two-day air, and so on)
- Where you are shipping from
- Where you are shipping to

Generally, buyers pay additional costs such as duty, taxes, and customs clearance fees upon receipt of the package. To understand all the ins and outs of international shipping, contact the USPS or the third-party shipping service you plan to use.

Calculating Package Weight

You don't want to guess the weight of a package when calculating postage or shipping fees at home. Overestimating the weight means you are paying more than you have to; underestimating means that the package may be returned to you, delaying delivery to the buyer. (In fact, if in doubt, it is best to overestimate the package rate.)

To be certain about a package's weight, you should purchase a shipping scale as part of your standard office equipment. You should make sure that you weigh *everything*, including the box and packaging materials. In fact, it's best to weigh an item *after* it's been completely prepared to go out the door.

Notify buyer of shipment

Keeping the buyer informed of what is happening at every stage of the purchasing process is key to customer satisfaction. And because customer satisfaction determines your feedback rating, which in turn will impact how many bidders will participate in your auctions and how much they will be willing to pay, nothing is more critical than sending out regular emails that make sure the buyer is kept up to date.

One of the most important emails you will send is the one notifying buyers that their items have shipped. When composing this email, include the following:

■ **The date on which you are shipping the item.** Don't fudge on this. If you make out the mailing label on Monday but don't actually get to the post office until Tuesday, make sure that Tuesday is the date you specify in your email. You might even want to include the exact time that you ship the item, as this can affect when, exactly, it will arrive at its destination.

- **The shipping carrier.** An essential piece of information, as it gives your buyer an idea of how the package will arrive: whether by special truck, their letter carrier, or by their having to go to a local package distribution center to pick it up—as is common in many rural areas.

- **The exact shipping terms.** Always specify whether the package has been shipped using standard USPS methods or a premium service such as Express (overnight) or Priority (two- or three-day delivery).

- **Insurance details.** If you have required that buyers purchase insurance on the item—or if they have personally requested that you add it onto the shipping costs—include all the details, including how much the item is insured for and what the insurance cost.

- **The approximate date (or range of dates) when it will arrive.** Although you may not be able to predict precisely when the package will be delivered, your carrier can usually provide a range during which the package is likely to arrive. Be especially careful when relaying this estimate during busy holiday mailing seasons, as there are few things that buyers are more sensitive about—or more likely to provide negative feedback about—than expecting their item by a certain date and not having it show up.

- **A routing number they can use to track the package.** If you use a premium shipping service or pay a small extra fee to the USPS, you can provide your buyer with a routing number and a website they can visit to track the progress of their package. This is an excellent way to enhance the customer experience for just a few extra pennies per package.

Follow up

After waiting the requisite number of days, you should send a follow-up email to buyers, asking them if they have received their item and are happy with it. Chances are good that if it hasn't arrived yet, or if the condition is not satisfactory, you would have heard from them already, but it's best to be proactive. After all, feedback becomes a permanent part of your record; despite the fact that there are mechanisms for mutually agreeing to remove the actual rating, the comments are permanent and can do the most damage to your reputation.

QUICK TIP

Pack with Care

Think twice before you stuff your shipping carton with yesterday's newspapers. Yes, your first priority is that the item arrive at its destination safe and undamaged, so do whatever it takes to assure that. But you should also consider the impression your buyers will get when they open the package. A sloppily or hastily packed box could reflect badly on you, whereas using tissue paper and ribbon and enclosing your business card or a personal note thanking a buyer for their business can go a long way toward convincing them they are dealing with a legitimate, high-quality seller. Their confidence in you will be reflected in their positive feedback and repeat business.

Ask for feedback

You can ask the buyer to submit feedback to eBay at the time that you send your follow-up email, or you can wait and send an email requesting this a day or two later. The latter is a good idea, because it gives the buyer a chance to respond to your initial message asking whether they are satisfied with the item, and it gives the impression that you are genuinely interested in their buying experience.

There should not be a hint of a "you-scratch-my-back-and-I'll-scratch-yours" offer to provide positive feedback when your buyers provide theirs. And under no circumstances should there be any hint of a threat or warning that failure to provide positive feedback could have negative ramifications.

An example of the type of note you should send:

Thank you for purchasing the <<item>>. Please provide me with feedback on the transaction and I will do the same for you.

Buyers have 90 days to provide feedback, and although it is to your advantage to have them give you positive feedback, you should *never* harass them to provide it, even if you notice that they have failed to do so. One polite email a week or two after the first one, reiterating your request, is acceptable, but more than that will be seen as intrusive and annoying, and could provoke a backlash.

QUICK TIP

Buy Insurance

If in doubt, buy shipping insurance for your item to cover the possibility that it will be lost or damaged in transit. The additional cost is negligible compared to the hassle of replacing the item—if it is even replaceable—or dealing with the fallout from negative feedback that an irate buyer may post.

Resolving Problems

No matter how conscientious and diligent you are, at some point something can go wrong. An item might break in transit. Or family matters or a busy spell may mean that you don't get the item packed and shipped when you promised in your listing.

More likely, the problem will be on the buyer's end. The buyer will be unhappy with the color of the dress described as "blue." Or surprised to find out that the radio was not in working order, even though your description said plainly that it was just being sold for parts. How far you are willing to go to accommodate buyers is one of the business decisions you must make as an eBay seller. Keep in mind that since they can post them publicly, the candid opinions of every single one of your buyers matter. So you may want to go the extra mile in your eBay business.

Have patience

Sometimes customers don't even know they're being rude. Perhaps, they're just not accustomed to using email for business correspondence. Or they might be poor typists and come off sounding brusque and unfriendly. Sometimes, of course, they *are* being rude. And it can really rankle you to have to deal with them. Say a buyer irritably demands the item just one day after the auction closes—before you've even had a chance to ship it. Or sends you a series of abrupt email messages quizzing you about an item they've already bought, as if they still have the option of backing out (according to eBay rules, they don't). Except in those cases where you feel that you are the target of a scam, you may want to just grin and bear it for the sake of your feedback rating. Of course, there will be times when that is simply not possible—you will lack the patience, or feel that a customer is being so unreasonable that your self-respect demands a stern response. How you act is your personal choice. Just be aware that with a rating system like eBay's, individual buyers wield a significant amount of power over your reputation.

However, if they've won your auction, your best strategy is to get the transaction over with—and only then, if you feel strongly enough about it, add that person's eBay member ID to your "blocked" list (see page 143). If you feel *really* strongly, you may want to leave negative feedback stating that the buyer was difficult to deal with, although there are risks involved in taking this step (see page 183).

If, however, you have an inkling that someone is going to be trouble before the auction ends, you should check out their eBay feedback rating. You may find out that they have caused other people trouble. And not just by being rude, either, but by not paying for auctions won or by leaving unearned negative criticism.

Pay attention when you see this—and rather than just letting it go, consider blocking that member from making further bids. If they already have the highest bid, and you worry that they might win, you can even take steps to have that bid removed by eBay. This is quite a drastic action, but it may be worthwhile under certain circumstances.

Quick Tip

Enough with the Shouting Already

Never compose a message in ALL CAPS when communicating with a buyer. Although you may be frustrated, or feel that the person on the other end of the email string is not getting your message, using all caps is the online equivalent of shouting at them—and that's no way to start a good business relationship.

Soothe the fears of newbies

You may find yourself answering very basic questions—not just about your item, but about eBay procedures in general. Or you may find yourself reassuring a potential buyer about things you'd already said in your listing. Try not to be annoyed—chances are good that you're dealing with a new arrival to eBay.

In such cases, be especially considerate! Although they may seem tentative, new buyers can be very enthusiastic about winning an item. Indeed, they might have been drawn to the eBay site specifically because they were looking for an item like the one you have listed—and to be even slightly impatient with them might have the effect of scaring off a legitimate, eager buyer who will come back again and again to your listings.

When in doubt, use the phone

Sometimes email isn't the best communication medium. You may choose to stick with it because it's easiest and because it protects your privacy, but—depending on the type of items you sell and the kind of follow-up support that you guarantee to your customers—you may also want to make use of the telephone to answer questions and keep in touch with your buyers.

In such cases, be respectful of your buyers' preferences as well. First, ask for permission to contact them by telephone and for the best number and most convenient times to call. Do not call many times or leave multiple messages in a row; always wait until they return your call before calling them back again. And some sellers believe it's a good idea to always send an email ahead of time, then follow up with a phone call, so as not to appear too intrusive.

Be careful about who you give your phone number to, especially if it's also your home number. And unless you've had your identity blocked on your phone, anyone with caller

ID will be able to get your number from their phone display—so keep that in mind when you are making calls from numbers that you don't necessarily want to be made public.

Is the customer always right?

It's often said that the customer is always right, but how far are you willing to go to prove that you mean it?

- What happens if a customer emails you that an item has arrived broken or damaged? (See page 176.)

- What if a customer complains that you didn't adequately describe the item in your listing description?

- What if a customer simply states that they don't like an item?

Situations like these are not uncommon when it comes to selling goods to others—especially those you will never meet face to face. And it's best to think ahead of time about how you will handle sticky situations—and put your conclusions into your auction listings or Seller FAQs rather than leaving any ambiguity.

It's a good idea to check out what other sellers—particularly the ones selling items in your particular category—say in their policy sections. Buyer expectations are often based on standard practices. For example, sellers of used laptop computers often offer 30-, 60-, or 90-day warranties for all parts excluding the battery. You might choose to guarantee the battery as well if you want to stand out in that category—or you may want to follow standard practice to minimize the chance that you will have to go to extra trouble and expense after the sale. How far you're willing to go to service customers is one of the biggest decisions you make when starting your eBay business.

Many sellers will state flatly that there are absolutely no returns allowed. Bidders are told to carefully examine the listing description as well as the photos to avoid any misunderstandings about the item in question. Other sellers won't ship items unless adequate insurance has been purchased (at the buyer's expense).

Others, taking the reverse strategy, promise satisfaction guaranteed and state their willingness to accept returns on anything the customer is not happy with. If you decide to go this route, keep in mind that a certain percentage of your customers are going to take you up on your offer! It might even make people less careful about bidding on your items. If they know they can return them, there's much less risk associated with being the winner. In such cases—especially if the items are larger or bulky—it makes sense to state that the buyer pays the shipping fees for any items returned.

The important thing to remember is that whatever business decisions you make will be reflected in your feedback rating. Although you don't have to roll over for every complaining customer, you will probably want to strike some sort of placating pose over minor issues to preserve your good reputation.

Lost or Damaged in Transit?

You've carefully packed and shipped an item—taking care to notify the buyer when it will arrive at their doorstep—and the buyer emails you to say it never arrived, or, alternatively, that it has arrived broken or damaged. What do you do?

Lacking other evidence that fraud is being attempted, most sellers will honor the buyer's demand for a refund or replacement. However to protect yourself and discourage dishonesty, you can take certain steps before sending the check or replacement product:

- **Check on the buyer's feedback rating.** Has the buyer attempted to do this to other sellers? A pattern of receiving supposedly broken items—or not receiving them at all—points either to extraordinarily bad luck or a less-than-ethical buyer.

- **Ask the buyer to return the broken item.** This will circumvent any hint of fraud, as buyers who have reported breakage hoping to retain the item in question will be immediately thwarted.

- **Ask the buyer to send a photograph of the broken item.** Again, this can help prevent fraud. If the item is too large or awkward to justify the expense of shipping it back to you, ask the buyer to provide a clear picture that shows the item has indeed been broken or damaged before you provide a refund or send another item.

- **Inform the buyer that you will be noting the details of the transaction—without a negative feedback score—in the feedback form.** Be very clear that this is not a threat that you will be providing negative feedback—indeed, you do not intend to provide anything that will impact a buyer's overall numerical score—but rather to explain in the "comments" field that there was a problem with the transaction that you subsequently fixed. This should keep buyers honest, as too much evidence that they have had bad experiences with breakage will warn other sellers off.

The eBay Feedback System

A fter a transaction has been successfully completed, you will be asked to leave comments on a public Web page that rates your experience with your buyer. They will be asked to do the same for you. The goal of this exchange is to keep the community a safe place to do business.

Nothing is more important to your standing within the eBay community than feedback. Numerous studies have shown that the higher your feedback rating, the more people bid on your auctions, and the higher end prices you get. Understanding how the feedback system works—and how to make sure that your rating stays as close to 100 percent positive as possible—is therefore key to your ability to make a success of your eBay business.

QUICK TIP

The Permanence of eBay Feedback

eBay feedback cannot be erased! This is why you must put in the extra effort to make sure your buyers are happy with every transaction.

What is the feedback system?

eBay's feedback system is made up of comments and ratings left by the members you've bought from and sold to. It is the largest user-generated rating system in the world. The fact that it works as well as it does speaks to the involvement and integrity of the overall eBay community. Although the system has some flaws (see page 183), it is the best method eBay has come up with for providing information about the reliability and reputation of individual buyers and sellers to each other.

All comments and ratings are publicly available on your user profile page for anyone who has your eBay member name. They are also displayed prominently next to your listing if someone clicks through on your auction title from the main search or category browser pages.

QUICK TIP

Building Your Reputation

eBay sellers with established reputations—either online or via traditional storefronts—can expect about 8 percent more revenue than new sellers marketing the same goods, a July 2006 University of Michigan study shows.

How the feedback system works

After a transaction is complete, your buyer (or the person who sold something to you) is invited to provide feedback on the experience. They have two ways of doing this: by checking a box from a menu that has "positive," "negative," and "neutral" options and by providing qualitative feedback in the form of written comments. They can use up to 88 characters to do this. eBay members are encouraged to provide feedback in both ways.

Whether you have bought or sold, you subsequently receive:

- +1 point for each positive comment.

- 0 points for each neutral comment.

- –1 point for each negative comment.

On each auction you list, and on your member profile, eBay will display a percentage that reflects the proportion of positive to neutral or negative points you have received, as well as (in parentheses) the total number of people who have provided you with feedback.

Thus "JohnSmith 98.7 percent (438)" means that the eBay member with the User ID JohnSmith has had feedback from 438 other members, and it has been positive 98.7 percent of the time.

Buyers are very interested in the feedback ratings of the sellers whose auctions they are considering bidding on—and take them very seriously. But as a seller, you should also be checking on the ratings of the people who are bidding on your listings, particularly if you are offering high-value items like cars or pricey antiques.

Detailed Seller Ratings

An eBay feature allows buyers to expand on the information they provide to other eBay members when giving feedback on a purchase. In addition to specifying the overall quality of their experience with a particular seller (positive, neutral, or negative) they can specifically rate the seller across four parameters:

- **Item as described.** Was the item represented accurately in the description and the photograph(s)? Were there any surprises when the item actually arrived?

- **Communication.** How well—and how quickly—did the seller respond to queries?

Advice on Feedback

On providing feedback:

- **Always do it.** It's your contribution to the community and it also makes eBay a safer place to do business, which is in your best interest.

- **Think carefully before providing your feedback.** Remember, your comments will appear on your buyers' (or sellers') permanent eBay records, and you want to be fair to them.

- **Remember that your buyers (or sellers) will also have a chance to provide feedback about _you_.** Like it or not, what you say could influence what they say. The possibility of "retaliatory" feedback is very real.

On receiving feedback:

- Although a high positive percentage feedback score is good for business, you should always check the comments for particulars. Your buyers will be looking at them, too, and it's best to be prepared for questions and concerns.

- Use the feedback comments as a way to improve your business tactics and customer service.

- Always try to resolve any problems with your buyers before they have a chance to leave (permanent) negative feedback.

The 90-Day Limit

You have 90 days to leave feedback for anyone you've had a transaction with. If you want to leave feedback for anyone you've had a transaction with more than 90 days prior, you may be able to use the "single transaction form" on the Leave Feedback page. However, whether your comment will be posted or not will be left up to the discretion of eBay.

- **Shipping time.** Did the buyer receive the item within a reasonable timeframe?

- **Shipping and handling charges.** Were these charges appropriate given the size and weight of the item?

eBay Detailed Seller Ratings are based on a star system, with five stars representing the highest level of satisfaction and one star the lowest. However, the Detailed Seller Ratings do not affect the seller's overall feedback score — that is still determined according to the positive/neutral/negative rating.

Removing feedback

In most cases, feedback cannot be removed. But eBay has put some measures in place to make sure the system is working fairly. Under certain very specific (and very unusual) circumstances, eBay will remove feedback.

It's important to understand that if you leave negative feedback for another eBay member, you could be held legally responsible for damages if you are sued and a court determines that your remarks are libelous or defame your transaction partner.

There are three circumstances under which eBay will remove feedback from your permanent record:

- A buyer includes your real name (not your eBay User ID) or telephone number in a comment on the feedback page.

- A buyer threatens — and follows through on those threats — to leave negative or neutral feedback for you unless you deliver additional items or related services not included in the original listing.

- You block a buyer with whom you have had a negative experience from bidding on items and, in order to circumvent that, the buyer signs up for a new eBay account under a different name and wins another one of your auctions with the primary purpose of being able to leave you retaliatory negative feedback. (You can only leave feedback for someone that you have had a transaction with.)

Mutual Feedback Withdrawal

Happily, there is a remedy if a buyer leaves negative feedback about you but you are later able to resolve the problem. This is called Mutual Feedback Withdrawal. It's important to understand that it's only a *partial* removal of the negative feedback that your buyer has submitted about you.

Say that a buyer is unhappy because an item arrived damaged in the mail and they have not been able to get hold of you because you've been on vacation. Once you understand the situation, you make it right by refunding the cost of the item—but not before the buyer has left an angry comment and given you a negative feedback score.

The Mutual Feedback Withdrawal process allows both you and your buyer to have the feedback *scores* related to that transaction deleted from your permanent records—and your feedback *percentage score* will increase proportionally. But it's critical to understand that the text comment itself will not be deleted, but will always be a part of your permanent record.

Because buyers pay attention to what others says as well as the total numerical score, this emphasizes the importance of working things out before any feedback at all has been provided. You must request Mutual Feedback Withdrawal within 30 days of receiving feedback, or within 90 days of the transaction date, whichever is later.

No Artificial Enhancement Allowed

eBay strictly forbids members to "scratch each others' backs" by engaging in transactions solely for the purpose of being able to leave positive feedback for one another that artificially inflates a seller's positive feedback ratings.

Reading the stars

Feedback stars are awarded to eBay members who have achieved 10 or more feedback points. The stars are displayed next to the member's User ID. Members receive:

■ +1 point for each positive comment and rating

■ 0 points for each neutral comment and rating.

■ –1 point for each negative comment and rating.

Each color represents a particular feedback level.

Yellow Star = 10 to 49 points

Blue Star = 50 to 99 points

Turquoise Star = 100 to 499 points

Purple Star = 500 to 999 points

Red Star = 1,000 to 4,999 points

Green Star = 5,000 to 9,999 points

Yellow Shooting Star = 10,000 to 24,999 points

Turquoise Shooting Star = 25,000 to 49,999 points

Purple Shooting Star = 50,000 to 99,999 points

Red Shooting Star = 100,000 or higher

Feedback Flaws

You may have noticed that, for the vast majority of your fellow eBay sellers, more than 99 percent of their feedback is positive. If you were grading on a curve, with a 99.8 percent rating as an "A," a rating of 97.5 percent would probably be equivalent to a grade of "C"—and it's relatively hard to find buyers with this low a rating. Below 96 percent—forget it. No one's going to touch your wares.

eBay and other proponents of the system point to these extremely high ratings as evidence that the community is policing itself as it should. The reason that sellers with poor ratings are so hard to find, they say, is that they are rapidly eliminated from the auction food chain. If they get bad ratings, they have trouble finding buyers, and so they go out of eBay business.

However, there's another interpretation to these extraordinarily high feedback ratings: the fear of retaliatory feedback. This occurs when a seller (or a buyer—it can happen on both sides) becomes angered by a negative comment posted about them, logs on, and posts a negative comment in return.

This is against eBay's rules of conduct. But since eBay has no way of determining the internal motivations of members posting negative comments, it can happen—and by certain estimates, it happens frequently—that innocent sellers' reputations suffer. Because reputation is everything on eBay, this kind of behavior results in very real financial losses.

Some observers claim that it is the threat of retaliatory feedback that is behind the fact that everyone seems so circumspect about leaving comments. Rather than risk a negative comment, many sellers would rather say nothing. And the way eBay is currently set up, you know how many people rated a particular buyer or seller, but you don't know how many people had transactions with this person but refrained from providing any feedback at all.

This might sound like a small point, but it's key. If most people are holding their tongues and simply not saying anything about the poor business ethics of a particular buyer, then that person's rating won't reflect reality.

eBay has argued time and time again that, despite its flaws, its rating system is the best device it can use to promote a safe and profitable transaction platform for its users. And despite the criticisms, no one has yet to come up with a better one.

Open Your eBay Store

"One of the smartest things you can do to boost your credibility is to open an eBay Store. This sends a signal to your buyers that you are serious about your eBay business and likely to be around for some time."

Christina Cousino,
BBB Member, eBay PowerSeller,
and owner of Foffun's Online Auctions,
Napoleon, Ohio

Beyond Auctions

eBay Stores

I f your auctions have been successful, you may want to graduate to an eBay Store. Just as with a real store, it's a way to get all your goods into a single place rather than having them scattered all over the site. If people like what you sell, they may be looking for more of the same. You can boost your aura of legitimacy as well, and keep your inventory on your virtual shelves for as long as 90 days.

If you take this step, you are making your first move into the world of e-tailing—a world that extends well beyond eBay. Although you may well choose to stick with eBay as your e-commerce platform, once many eBay sellers get a taste for running an online store, they then make the transition to building their own retail sites on the Web, thus expanding their businesses beyond anything they could ever have imagined when they listed their first eBay auction.

What is an eBay Store?

Beginning in 2002, eBay began offering its sellers something new: the option of opening dedicated storefronts that allowed them to take advantage of its vast technology infrastructure and global customer base through their own dedicated stores.

What eBay offers through its eBay Stores service are the tools you need to build your online store without having to start from scratch. These include hosting (where your online store resides physically), helping you design and build your site (for which you'd otherwise have to go to a Web designer), shopping carts (how your customers gather up the products they want to buy), and payment functionality that helps your customers successfully check out once

Naming Your Store

Choosing a store name is one of the most critical things you will do. Not only must it contain relevant words that will allow search engines—eBay's and others—to find you, but it will be used to create your URL, or Web address. As always, think like a buyer: what words are the most direct, the most commonly used, and the most descriptive of the products or services you sell? If you sell office supplies at a discount, naming your store Discount Office Supplies is your best bet. Of course, your ideal name might already be taken, so you might have to try several combinations before you find something that works. And whatever you choose, it will be incorporated into your URL—for example: *http://stores. ebay.com/Discount-Office-Supplies*. If you already have a brick-and-mortar store, it would be best to name your eBay Store the same thing if possible. (Sometimes this isn't possible, if the name has already been taken by another eBay member.)

they've selected their items. Of course, because eBay Stores are a service, you'll pay a monthly fee for the privilege of accessing their features.

An eBay Store allows you to consolidate all your sales—Fixed Price as well as auctions—in one place. And the main benefits include the ability to promote your sales more effectively and to get to know your buyers much more intimately. The stores can be easily customized to have the look and feel you desire, so you can start establishing your own brand.

Another of the major advantages is that you get your very own Web address, so if you decide to market your store and/or advertise outside eBay, you can direct potential buyers straight to your store, without them having to enter through eBay. This makes it less likely that they'll see your competition when they come looking for you.

All in all, eBay Stores provides you with a safe and highly structured environment to make your foray into e-commerce.

When to open a store

eBay will not allow you to open a store right away. You must first hold enough auctions to get a minimum of 20 buyers to comment favorably on your ability to deliver satisfaction before you are eligible.

To open an eBay Store, you must have:

- **A seller's account on eBay.**

- **A feedback score of 20 or more.** You need to get at least 20 buyers to provide you with positive feedback before you will be allowed to proceed.

- **Be "ID Verified."** The ID Verify system establishes proof of an eBay member's identity, helping both buyers and sellers trust each other (see page 190).

Creating Relevant Categories

When you open an eBay Store, you no longer have to depend on the predefined categories and subcategories provided by eBay; you can create ones that best suit your offerings. Creating your own categories is one of the most effective ways you can help buyers to find you by using searches, either on eBay or on the Web.

You do this by putting the most direct, relevant descriptive words into your category titles. If you sell designer shoes, first create a store name that states that directly. Then, create categories that state specifically what you are selling—a Prada category, for example. Finally, create subcategories that are even more specific— such as "red Prada shoes." That way, anyone searching for red Prada shoes will go directly to all of your listings.

■ **Have a PayPal account.** PayPal is an e-commerce payment service that allows payments to be safely made through the Internet. Most sellers on eBay accept PayPal as a payment option for items won in auctions; many will *only* accept PayPal.

There are also a number of business conditions that will tell you that the time is right to open an eBay Store. You may notice that you are getting a number of regular customers who are requesting that you put all your auctions into a single location. You may have found a steady, reliable source of inventory and want to offer a mix of Fixed Price and auction items to suit the needs of a range of different types of buyers. Or you might be considering building your own website independent of eBay and want to start under "protected" and safe circumstances within the eBay marketplace to give you experience before you go out into the wild Web.

The advantages of an eBay Store

There are a number of benefits to opening your own eBay Store:

■ **You can create your own brand.** For any business, forging a unique identity is an essential step toward developing long-term loyalty among customers. Having an eBay Store helps you to create your own business identity, possibly with its own unique look and feel. Although eBay provides you with a number of design templates, you still have choices about color, the graphics you put on your site—including your own logo—and other content. Although eBay tools make it easy to get your site up, some sellers, rather than working with the standard eBay templates, go to an independent designer to create a truly unique look.

■ **Keep your items on display longer.** By using eBay's Store Inventory format, you can keep your Buy It Now items displayed for longer periods of time.

■ **Create your own categories.** If your items don't fall neatly into any of eBay's own categories and subcategories, you can make your own. This will help buyers understand at a glance the type of products or services you have to offer.

■ **Enable buyers to search within your eBay Store only.** This very valuable feature allows anyone who is interested in the type of items you have for sale to do a search within your items only. This means that, rather than getting search results that include items from throughout eBay (including from your competition), the search page will only display your items.

■ **Cross-promote your items.** When a potential buyer clicks on one of your items, your other items will appear at the bottom of the page.

■ **Get a unique Web address (URL).** If you're going to try to attract buyers from outside the eBay community, you will need your own Web address so that people on the Web can go directly to your eBay Store without having to be eBay members.

■ **Get access to site traffic reports.** One of the more valuable tools that eBay provides to its store owners is the ability to see exactly how many people have been visiting your auction or Fixed Price items. This will help you determine whether you've written effective titles and descriptions and give you feedback on whether you need to modify them.

ID Verified

In addition to your all-important feedback rating, there are other ways to establish trust as a seller. One of those ways is to become "ID Verified," which means you have established proof of your identity with eBay. After you're successfully verified, other eBay members will see an ID Verify icon in your feedback profile. In the ID Verify process, a third-party company (Equifax in the United States) works with eBay to confirm members' identity by cross-checking their contact information against consumer and business databases.

Obviously, the biggest advantage of being ID Verified is that it increases buyers' confidence and trust in you. This is likely to increase both the number of bids and the prices you'll receive. In addition, once your identity has been verified, you can:

■ List items offering Buy It Now or Best Offer options.

■ List using the Multiple Item format, which allows you to list identical multiple items together in an online auction. The winning bid in a Multiple Item listing is based on the highest bid *per item*.

■ List items under the Fixed Price format, which allows you to list multiple, identical items in one listing, with a fixed price for each item. Buyers can choose the quantity they want and pay the set price. For example, say you have acquired 100 packages of 200 three-inch aluminum nails and want to sell them for $2.99 per package. You list them with a quantity of 100 and a price of $2.99. Buyers can request any quantity they like at that price.

■ Buy items priced over $15,000 with Buy It Now.

■ Bid above $15,000 on regular auctions.

■ Bid on eBay Live Auctions, which allow you to bid in real time on auctions taking place on the floors of auction houses around the globe. You can place absentee bids, bid live, or watch the auction online.

■ Sell in eBay's Mature Audiences category. Materials that are adult in nature or otherwise not appropriate for minors under 18 years of age cannot be listed on the main eBay site.

To be ID Verified you must be a resident of the United States or U.S. territories and pay a $5.00 application fee. The fee is returned if you are not verified after the background check is complete.

QUICK TIP

The eBay Store Icon

When you open an eBay Store, you will get a red door icon displayed next to your seller's User ID. Buyers who like what you have to offer in your auctions or Buy It Now listings can click on it and enter your store immediately to see what else you are selling.

The challenges of an eBay Store

Although there are many advantages to opening an eBay Store, you must decide whether doing this will fit in with your business and lifestyle goals. Among the challenges:

- **Increased costs.** You may need to take on more staff, spend more on travel to source goods, or spend more on packaging and shipping materials.

- **Increased customer demands.** Buyers expect more from eBay Store owners than from standard auction listers. They assume that you are devoting more time and resources to your business, and they will therefore want prompter responses to queries—and more professional treatment throughout the sales process in general.

- **Additional time requirements.** Because of these increased customer expectations, you will need to put in more time monitoring your auction and Fixed Price sales activities. You will probably have a higher volume of sales as well, which will cause the demands of your eBay business to increase.

- **The need for constant sourcing.** Imagine if you walked into a brick-and-mortar store and it was devoid of merchandise. It's the same with an online store. If eBay members click on your store icon, they expect to see items for sale. Sporadic listings are therefore not an option. You must have plenty of stock on your online shelves at all times. Expect to spend more time searching for items to put up for sale.

- **More competition.** Competition on eBay is fierce. You've probably noticed this with your auctions: there are other sellers putting up similar items with fixed prices that are lower than yours, and auctions with starting prices that undercut yours. This will just intensify when you open your eBay Store. Expect any new or exciting ideas or designs that you put up to be emulated by others. You must constantly innovate to succeed.

Store Options and Features

S etting up an eBay Store couldn't be easier. You click on the Sell tab on the home page and select "Seller Tools and eBay Stores." This will take you to a page that will invite you to set up an eBay Store. You will be prompted to create a store name and choose what kind of store you want (see page 193). If you fulfill the basic conditions for the store, you will be asked to accept the software license agreement, and you are ready to begin customizing your store immediately! If you haven't been ID Verified or don't have a PayPal account associated with your eBay member name, you will be prompted to fulfill these requirements before continuing. All charges will be applied to your credit card on file.

eBay Store options

One of the chief advantages of opening an eBay Store is that it is a relatively painless and safe way to enter the larger world of Web-based e-commerce. The tools are easy to use and don't require any technical knowledge to learn; because

QUICK TIP

Worth a Thousand Words

Use lots of graphics and photos when building your store. And keep your text content as brief as possible. Web surfers have notoriously short attention spans; you need to grab them with attractive graphics and short and snappy words.

all your choices are in the form of pre-formed templates and carefully structured options, you can literally get up and running in minutes.

There are three kinds of eBay Stores to choose from, all of which charge a fixed monthly subscription rate to set up and operate:

- **Basic Store.** This is the fundamental—and least expensive—option, providing sellers who are just starting out with an easy way to get their online retail store up and running. You get access to eBay's Selling Manager tool to help you track your listings (see page 194), five customizable store pages, and up to 300 categories in which to list your products. eBay customer support is available Monday through Friday, from 6 a.m. to 6 p.m., if you run into any problems. Customer support reps will answer questions about how the tools work, walk you through the processes of setting up and customizing your store, and help you manage your products/listings.

- **Feature Store.** This option comes with more selling tools. You get more, and better, choices for customizing your site, and 10 pages to display your wares. The Selling Manager Pro (see page 194) tool comes free with your monthly subscription fee, and you have access to more advanced traffic tracking and management capabilities than if you merely subscribe to the basic store—for example, you get to see where your buyers are coming from on the Web before they land at your eBay Store.

- **Anchor Store.** This most advanced option is for sellers—usually PowerSellers—who have a very high volume of sales and need special capabilities and tools to help them manage that volume. With an Anchor store you get dedicated 24-hour support, as well as 15 pages on which you can showcase your products, among other additional functionality.

Leverage Picture Manager

Picture Manager is eBay's own picture subscription service (there are other, third-party services that do the same thing—some charge less than eBay). Rather than uploading individual pictures for each item, Picture Manager lets you upload all your photos into a "library" that you can use as you want when putting together your item listings. This helps you avoid the per-photo upload fees that eBay ordinarily charges.

All eBay Store owners automatically get one megabyte of Picture Manager storage space, which allows you to store everything from logos to design elements for your eBay Store to photos for your auctions.

Turbo Lister

If your volume of transactions starts growing and you are finding it difficult to manage, you should consider using Turbo Lister. Turbo Lister is a free eBay tool that lets you create all your listings offline and then upload them all at the same time. This can save you enormous amounts of time, as you won't have to go through the standard listing screen every time you have a new item to put up for sale or auction. Designed for medium to high volume sellers, Turbo Lister also gives you access to a wide number of features, including the ability to change characteristics on all your listings at once. For example, say you decide to freshen up the design of your listings by changing the colors or enlarging your logo. You can do this simultaneously for all your listings. If you put a credit card on file with eBay, you can also schedule your items to go online at specific times.

eBay Store features

Selling Manager and Selling Manager Pro

Selling Manager is a tool that allows you to manage all your eBay activities from one place. You will be able to track listings as well as monitor all feedback, email, and payments from this single place, rather than having to navigate the eBay site to perform the various tasks.

Selling Manager Pro is a more advanced version of Selling Manager that allows you to track your inventory—a very valuable thing—list items in bulk, send bulk feedback and emails to customers, and build reports on various aspects of your business, such as whether you are operating at a profit or a loss. Some of the other features of Selling Manager Pro:

- **Track the status of your completed auctions.** There are some basic but essential steps you need to take after your auctions have closed, such as contacting the buyer, acknowledging payment, and actually shipping items. This feature helps you stay on top of these things so that your post-auction activities are successfully completed.

- **Create customized email templates.** Rather than having to reinvent the wheel every time you send out an email to a customer, this feature allows you to build templates that you can reuse every time you interact with buyers. For example, you can have a template for an email you send every time someone has won an auction; one reminding buyers to submit feedback; and one notifying them that an item has been shipped.

- **Relist multiple sold and unsold listings immediately.** If an auction fails, and you want to relist your item, Selling Manager Pro will do it automatically.

- **Manage unpaid auctions.** This feature allows you to track which payments have not arrived, and lists the steps you need to take if a buyer refuses to pay or is nonresponsive.

Custom Pages

A "page" on the Web is a single screen full of content that displays graphics and text, and you have 5, 10, or 15 of them depending on the type of eBay Store you are subscribed to (see page 196). You can always buy more pages from eBay. Think of your custom pages as your storefront windows. You can design pages that showcase specific products, your store, or even your personal history. The more keywords you can put on your pages that are relevant to your business, the more easily buyers on eBay—as well as on the Web—can find you.

eBay provides you with design templates that make it easy to create pages that reflect your brand. As always, however, you can go outside eBay to get more unique designs for your pages, and as you build your business, and strengthen your brand, you may want to do this.

Store Traffic Reports

eBay's Traffic Reports feature is free with your subscription and gives you detailed data about your store's traffic. You can access data on:

- All pages within your store, including any custom pages, custom category pages, and search.

- All item pages regardless of format (auctions, Fixed Price, Store Inventory).

- Other pages on eBay that are specific to you as a seller, including your Seller's Other Items page, your Feedback page, and your About Me page.

- Other pages associated with your listings, such as bid and Buy It Now confirmation pages that only buyers see.

QUICK TIP

Start Small
Given the way that eBay Stores subscriptions are structured, there is no risk to starting with the Basic Store and upgrading gradually to the premium services as your business expands.

Your Traffic Reports are categorized as follows:

- **Traffic reports.** These tell you the total number of visitors to all your pages, so you can see which ones were the most popular. You can also see where your visitors came from: whether from within eBay or from another website.

- **Path reports.** These help you understand exactly how your visitors behaved when they came to your store: how and where they entered, as well as the last page they visited before exiting your store.

- **Bidding and Buying reports.** With these reports, you can see which listings succeeded—and which didn't—as well as the sites and keywords that resulted in the most bids.

eBay Store Options and Features

OPTION	BASIC STORE	FEATURE STORE	ANCHOR STORE
Customer Support	Monday through Friday, 6 a.m.–6 p.m. (Pacific time)	Monday through Friday, 6 a.m.–6 p.m. (Pacific time)	Unlimited dedicated 24-hour support
Custom pages	5 pages	10 pages	15 pages
Store categories	300	300	300
Selling management tools	Selling Manager	Selling Manager Pro	Selling Manager Pro
Store name appears in "Shop eBay Stores" area of matching search results	Occasionally	Sometimes	Frequently
Picture Manager	1 megabyte free	1 megabyte free and $5 off subscription	1 gigabyte free plus free subscription
Rotating promotional placement on eBay Stores gateway	N/A	Text link in the center of the page	Store logo at the top of the page
Email marketing (newsletters and promotional emails)	5,000 emails/month	5,000 emails/month	5,000 emails/month
Traffic reports	N/A	Advanced	Advanced

eBay Express

eBay Express offers qualified sellers the opportunity to sell items at fixed Buy It Now prices in a "consolidated" marketplace that includes offerings from a broad range of other eBay sellers. What's important to understand about eBay Express is that it's all about *buyer convenience*: it is specially designed to appeal to buyers who might be too anxious—or impatient—to participate in traditional auctions. The advantage to you, the seller: access to a broader range of would-be customers than you might have through straight auctions or your eBay Store.

There are a number of buyer advantages to shopping eBay Express. For starters, there's instant gratification: there are no auctions here, only set prices, so buyers can get their hands on goods immediately. No waiting for an auction to close—and no uncertainty about whether they will actually get a desired item.

Also, there is a streamlined checkout procedure. An eBay Store is like having your own storefront: just as in a brick-and-mortar store, customers "enter" and "exit" virtually—by following links, of course, rather than by physically walking through the door—and they check out their items by paying you, the store owner, directly.

With eBay Express, however, it's as if you're offering your wares in a virtual market with just one checkout stand. Buyers can pick and choose from among all the merchandise displayed by thousands of sellers and can pay for everything with a single PayPal or credit card transaction. No need to send emails to and from individual sellers or send separate PayPal payments to each seller.

As an added advantage for buyers, every eBay Express transaction is covered by a Buyer Protection program that will refund the price of the purchase in full if a buyer doesn't receive an ordered item or it turns out to be different than advertised. As well, buyers can "chat" electronically with live customer service representatives anytime just by clicking on a mouse.

For sellers, eBay Express offers two chief advantages: the marketplace itself is bigger, as it includes potential buyers who might otherwise shun auction-style listings, and you get paid more quickly—and with fewer hassles—than if you were dealing with buyers individually.

Selling on eBay Express is easy—all you have to do is meet the minimal qualifications (have a feedback rating of at least 100, at least 98 percent of it positive); list your items using a Fixed Price, Store Inventory, or Buy it Now format that includes a photo, lists the item's condition (new, used, refurbished), and shipping costs; and become a PayPal Premier or PayPal Business merchant (see page 66). You must also be a U.S.-registered seller, and the items you are selling must be located in the United States.

If you meet all the above criteria, there is one additional step you must take before your items will be automatically listed on eBay Express: allow buyers to purchase multiple items with single payments. You do this by going to your Preferences page within My eBay. Under the "Combined payments and shipping discounts" section, you will see this option. Select it, and you're done—it's automatic! There are no other steps required on your end: your items will automatically appear on the regular eBay site as well as on eBay Express.

Promoting Your Store

There are a number of ways that you can promote your eBay Store, both from within and from outside eBay. Inside eBay, you have the Cross-Promotion tools, for example, that allow you to entice browsers of one of your auctions to your eBay Store. Outside of eBay, you can use standard search engine optimization (SEO) techniques to attempt to boost your Google or Yahoo search ranking. And eBay has special tools to help you create marketing aids such as business cards and brochures. Here's what you can do to increase the traffic at your eBay Store.

- **Drive traffic to your Store Inventory items by cross-promoting them.** It can be difficult to attract buyers to your Store Inventory listings, as they will only appear on search pages after all auction and Fixed Price listings. Use cross-promotion techniques (see page 200) on your other listings to drive eBay buyers to your Store Inventory listings.

- **Offer a variety of selling formats.** The eBay community likes variety. Some buyers love the thrill of a competitive auction; others want simply to buy what they

QUICK TIP

Link Listing Headings to Your eBay Store

Remember, it's important to link to your eBay Store pages wherever possible. The best place to do this is in your auction listings—especially in the headings.

want—*now*. That's why, rather than holding nothing but traditional auctions or offering only Fixed Price format listings, eBay PowerSellers recommend having an eBay Store with a variety of formats: auction style as well as Buy it Now or Store Inventory.

■ **Choose the right format to match your type of merchandise.** Different listing formats are appropriate for different kinds of items. Store Inventory or Fixed Price formats are best for run of the mill items, the auction format is effective for unusual or unique items, and Fixed Price or Store Inventory works well for brand new items. Additionally, exciting items you feel will create a "buzz" should always be listed in the auction format. And those items that are less likely to attract a lot of attention from a lot of buyers should be listed as Store Inventory.

■ **Drive buyers from auction formats to similar multiple Store Inventory listings.** You might have a large assortment of radios of different makes, manufacturers, and models. By listing one radio in an auction or Fixed Price listing, you can use cross-promotion to send buyers interested in radios to your eBay Store.

■ **Promote multiple quantity items.** Likewise, you might have 200 sets of king-size linen bedsheets. Because you can list all of them as Store Inventory for one very low price for an entire month, you could run an auction listing one of them and use it to direct potential buyers to your eBay Store, where you can offer the rest of your inventory for a Fixed Price.

■ **Do your research.** eBay Marketplace Research will help you analyze the listing formats that work best for the type of items that you sell.

Be Flexible in Your eBay Listing Strategy

The eBay community is constantly evolving, and other sellers will be on top of anything you do that works before you realize it. Constantly re-evaluate your strategy for listing the various kinds of items in your store, and check your traffic reports to see the results of any changes you make.

Minimize the eBay Header

When you subscribe to a Featured Store, you have the opportunity to shrink the eBay header on your store pages down to a minimum size, which allows you to emphasize your own logo and feature your own "brand" over the eBay one.

Store Referral Credit

One good reason for trying to drive traffic to your site from outside eBay, other than the additional revenues you'll reap, is that you'll get a refund of 75 percent of your Final Value Fees for any Store Inventory sale originating from a site other than eBay. There are some ground rules for qualifying for what is called the Store Referral Credit:

- The buyer must come to your eBay Store *directly* from a website outside eBay (that is, "*ebay.com*" doesn't appear in the website's URL).

- The buyer must come to your store because you've done something to promote it outside eBay.

- The buyer's Web browser must accept "cookies," which are pieces of code that websites place on visitors' computers that identify them if they come back.

- Buyers must purchase items during the same "session" in which they have entered your eBay Store.

Cross-promotions

One of your most powerful marketing tools is your ability to cross-promote your items no matter what format you use to sell them.

The concept behind cross-promotion is a basic one: every time someone takes an action that indicates interest in or curiosity about one of your items, you can have the eBay system display other items they can buy from you. This can happen when a would-be buyer views a listing, bids on an item, wins your item, or any combination of the three. You can allow eBay to automatically choose the items—up to 12—that will display at the bottom of the cross-promotion page, or you can decide for yourself which items to promote. You can also program "rules" for cross-promotion. For example, you can specify that anytime someone views, bids on, or wins an auction for an iPod or other digital music player, promotions for related accessories are displayed.

There are two main ways in which cross-promotion can help boost your eBay business:

- **You sell more items to your existing customers.** If your eBay business is based around a specific type of product or service—as most of them are—it's logical that someone who buys one of your items is going to be interested in others. By reminding them of what else you're offering, you have the potential to "hook" them into additional purchases.

- **You sell more expensive items.** You can tempt your existing customers to buy pricier items—this is called "upselling"—once you know what they are interested in.

Other promotional tools

- **Customize listing frames.** A "listing frame" is the combination of text and graphics that appear on every listing page. By opening an eBay Store, you gain the ability to customize the frame and use it to send more people to your eBay Store. The frame can include such things as your store name, a link to your store's home page, your logo, a search box that allows buyers to search your store, and a place for buyers to sign up for promotional email newsletters.

HTML Builder

Even if you don't have any HTML knowledge or experience, you can use eBay's HTML Builder to drive buyers to your store from your eBay listings, other Web pages, and promotional emails.

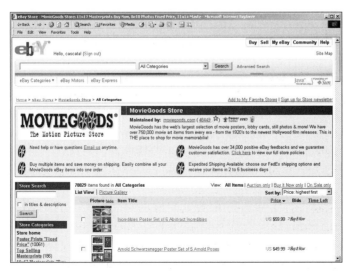

A customized listing frame.

■ **Create effective listing headers.** A "listing header" is a banner that appears on every page of your eBay Store. You can provide links to up to five of your categories there.

■ **Optimize search engine keywords.** The major search engines look for keywords embedded in Web pages to determine which ones are most appropriate to a particular search. You can—and should—customize the keywords for each of your eBay Store pages. Keywords, like the titles and descriptions you craft for individual items, should be direct and relevant, and include the obvious words that people would think of when describing your items. Try to think the way a person about to use a search engine would think, rather than as a marketer. Avoid flashy adjectives in favor of plain-spoken, ordinary language that would be used by your customers.

■ **Jump into email marketing.** Newsletters are a time-honored to keep in touch with your customers, keep them informed about what's going on, offer discounts or other promotions, and otherwise make sure that the name of your business stays fresh in their minds. Your eBay Stores subscription fee allows you to send out email newsletters to up to 5,000 of your buyers every month. eBay provides templates that allow you to put together a standard email newsletter quickly and easily; if you want a more distinctive look, you can build your own using an independent designer (or do it yourself if you know HTML).

■ **Use print materials.** Don't discount the power of printed promotional materials for your online store. Include a business card, brochure, or flyer in each and every shipment. Not only does this give customers your direct URL so they can come to your store from anywhere on the Web—thus earning you Store Referral Credits—it also gives them something to put on their bulletin boards or in their Rolodexes to refer to the next time they are shopping for an item similar to what you offered.

eBay offers you templates to create promotional flyers that can include your eBay Store header, a "theme"— you can design your own, or use one of eBay's—a custom message, and details about the purchase.

As an eBay Store seller, you also get access to templates for business cards, letterhead, and envelopes. Once you create any of these items, you can print them out as many times as you want.

■ **Register your domain name.** Create a store URL that's easy for buyers to remember by registering a domain name (for example, *www.superfancyclocks.com*). A buyer who types your domain name into their browser will be automatically forwarded to your store's home page.

Hook Customers with Low Prices

A very low starting price on an attractive item—say, between one cent and 99 cents—can generate a lot of traffic that you can then divert to your eBay Store using cross-promotion techniques.

Index

E

Acknowledgments

The Planning Shop would like to thank the staff of the Council of Better Business Bureaus and members of local Better Business Bureaus for their invaluable assistance:

- Steven Cole, President and CEO, Council of Better Business Bureaus
- Steve Cox, Vice President of Communications, Council of Better Business Bureaus
- Sheila Adkins, Director, Public Affairs, Council of Better Business Bureaus
- Ron Berry, Senior Vice President, Bureau Services Division, Council of Better Business Bureaus
- Steve Salter, Vice President, BBBOnLine
- Sally Munn, Vice President, Marketing & Membership Development, Council of Better Business Bureaus
- Fred Elsberry, President & CEO, BBB of Metro Atlanta, Athens, and Northeast Georgia
- Gary Almond, General Manager, BBB of Los Angeles County, Orange County, Riverside County, and San Bernardino County
- Tim Johnston, President & CEO, BBB of Northern Nevada
- Tricia Rossi, Operations Manager, BBB of Eastern Massachusetts, Maine, and Vermont
- Matthew Felling, President & CEO, BBB of Central and Northern Arizona
- James Baumhart, President & CEO, BBB of Chicago and Northern Illinois
- Kip Morse, President & General Manager, BBB of Central Ohio
- Katie Young, Director of Marketing & Communications, BBB of Alaska, Oregon, and Western Washington
- Charlie Mattingly, President & CEO, BBB of Louisville, Kentucky

Alice LaPlante would like to thank the following for their insight and expertise:

- Robert Britton, BBB member, eBay PowerSeller, and owner of Sterling Trading, Whitmore Lake, Michigan

- Chad Bryant, BBB member, eBay PowerSeller, and owner of RedRaven Press, Windsor, Colorado

- Deming Colbert, BBB member, eBay PowerSeller and owner of Puredeming.com, Denver, Colorado

- Christina Cousino, BBB member, eBay PowerSeller, and owner of Foffun's Online Auctions, Napoleon, Ohio

- Stella Kleiman, BBB member, eBay PowerSeller, and owner of FoundValue, San Francisco

- Chris Lawler, BBB member, eBay PowerSeller, and owner of Redlaw Motors, Fort Wayne, Indiana

- Zain Naboulsi, BBB member, eBay PowerSeller, and owner of Insert Knowledge Here, Mansfield, Texas

- Jim Nieciecki, BBB member, eBay PowerSeller, and owner of Federation Toys, Hoffman Estates, Illinois

- Jonathan Rosen, BBB member and CEO of Reliabid, Arlington, Virginia

- Craig Smith, BBB member, eBay PowerSeller, and president and owner of AutoAccessory4u.com, Corona, California

Every member of The Planning Shop's extended team is dedicated to producing the highest quality products and brings a special talent that enables us to develop thorough, practical, helpful, and graphically appealing books and business tools:

- Rhonda Abrams, Founder and CEO
- Maggie Canon, Managing Editor
- Mireille Majoor, Editorial Project Manager
- Deborah Kaye, Director of Academic Sales
- Rosa Whitten, Office Manager
- Diana Van Winkle, Graphic Designer
- Alice LaPlante, Writer
- Lloyd Davis, Copyeditor
- Kathryn Dean, Proofreader and Indexer
- Bridgett Novak, Contributing Editor
- Arthur Wait, Design and Technology Consultant
- Cosmo, Chief Canine Companion

The latest business tips, trends, and insights...

...all in The Planning Shop's free monthly email newsletter!

Want to stay on top of the latest trends in marketing, sales, and management? Looking for tips and advice that make you more effective, competitive, and profitable? Check out The Planning Shop Report, a free email newsletter from Rhonda Abrams and The Planning Shop.

Sign up for *free* at www.PlanningShop.com

Grow Your Business with The Planning Shop!

We offer a full complement of books and tools to help you build your business **successfully**.

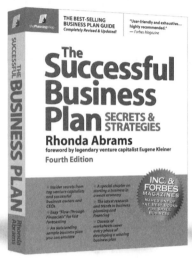

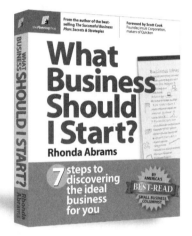

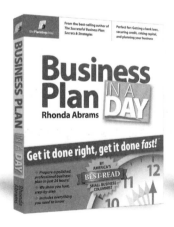

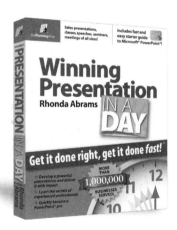

Ask your bookseller about these titles or visit www.PlanningShop.com

There's more where this book came from!